TIME ZONES

THIRD EDITION

JENNIFER WILKIN
CATHERINE FRAZIER
RICHARD FRAZIER
CARMELLA LIESKE

NATIONAL
GEOGRAPHIC
LEARNING

Australia • Brazil • Mexico • Singapore • United Kingdom • United States

NATIONAL GEOGRAPHIC
L E A R N I N G

National Geographic Learning,
a Cengage Company

Time Zones 2 Third Edition

Jennifer Wilkin, Catherine Frazier, Richard Frazier, and Carmella Lieske

Publisher: Andrew Robinson

Managing Editor: Derek Mackrell

Editorial Assistant: Elaine Lum

Director of Global Marketing: Ian Martin

Senior Product Marketing Manager: Anders Bylund

Heads of Regional Marketing:
    Charlotte Ellis (Europe, Middle East and Africa)
    Kiel Hamm (Asia)
    Irina Pereyra (Latin America)

Senior Production Controller: Tan Jin Hock

Associate Media Researcher: Jeffrey Millies

Senior Designer: Lisa Trager

Operations Support: Rebecca G. Barbush,
    Hayley Chwazik-Gee

Manufacturing Planner: Mary Beth Hennebury

Composition: Symmetry Creative Production, Inc.

For permission to use material from this text or product,
submit all requests online at **cengage.com/permissions**
Further permissions questions can be emailed to
permissionrequest@cengage.com

Student's Book with Online Practice
ISBN-13: 978-0-357-42169-7

Student's Book
ISBN-13: 978-0-357-41892-5

National Geographic Learning
200 Pier 4 Boulevard
Boston, MA 02210
USA

Locate your local office at **international.cengage.com/region**

Visit National Geographic Learning online at **ELTNGL.com**
Visit our corporate website at **www.cengage.com**

Printed in Mexico
Print Number: 03   Print Year: 2021

CONTENTS

SCOPE AND SEQUENCE

UNIT	FUNCTIONS	GRAMMAR	VOCABULARY	PRONUNCIATION	READ, WRITE, & WATCH
7 WHAT'S FOR DINNER?					PAGE 78
	Identifying things in the kitchen Expressing quantity **Real English:** *I can't wait!*	**Talking about countable and uncountable things:** *There's some* *There isn't any* *There are some* *There aren't any*	Food Utensils Things in the kitchen Adjectives to describe taste	Linked sounds	**Reading:** A Slice of History **Writing:** Text message **Video:** How Do We Taste Food?
8 YOU SHOULD SEE A DOCTOR!					PAGE 90
	Talking about health-related problems Asking for and giving advice **Real English:** *Come on!*	**Asking for and giving advice:** *What should I do?* *You should stay home and rest.* *You shouldn't go to school.* *Why don't you take some medicine?*	Health Injuries Parts of the body Verbs related to health	*Should, could, would*	**Reading:** Old New Medicines **Writing:** Article **Video:** Biking in Cities
9 I OFTEN SKATE AFTER SCHOOL					PAGE 102
	Talking about daily routines and activities **Real English:** *Good question.*	**Comparing present progressive and simple present:** *I am studying in school.* *I always study in school.* **Adverbs of frequency:** *rarely, once in a while, hardly ever*	Daily routines Habits Verbs related to traveling	Homophones	**Reading:** Unusual Commutes **Writing:** Descriptive paragraph **Video:** Helping Children to Love Nature
10 HOW DO YOU GET TO THE RESTAURANT?					PAGE 114
	Identifying places in the city **Real English:** *No problem.*	**Asking and giving directions:** *Where's the museum?* *How do you get to the park?* *Go straight down this street.* *Turn left./Make a right.* **Prepositions of place:** *behind, between, across from, in front of, next to, on the corner of*	Places in the city Directions Linking words	*O* sounds	**Reading:** Wayfinding Technology **Writing:** Text message **Video:** Shape of Cities
11 WHAT WERE YOU DOING?					PAGE 126
	Describing past experiences **Real English:** *Hurry up!*	**Comparing past progressive and simple past:** *Were you eating when she called?* *What were you doing last night?* *I was going down the stairs when I fell.*	Risk Adventure Homonyms	Ending blends: *-sk, -st, -nk, -nt*	**Reading:** Diving with Sharks **Writing:** Descriptive paragraph **Video:** The Misinformation Effect
12 WE'RE GOING TO VOLUNTEER!					PAGE 138
	Talking about future plans Talking about volunteering and charity events **Real English:** *Definitely!*	**Future with simple present:** *I'm going to volunteer.* *What are you going to do?* *When is the charity fair?* *The charity event is tomorrow.*	Charity events Volunteering Community service Nouns related to food	Reduction: *going to*	**Reading:** The "Ugly" Food Challenge **Writing:** Article **Video:** Feeding the 5,000

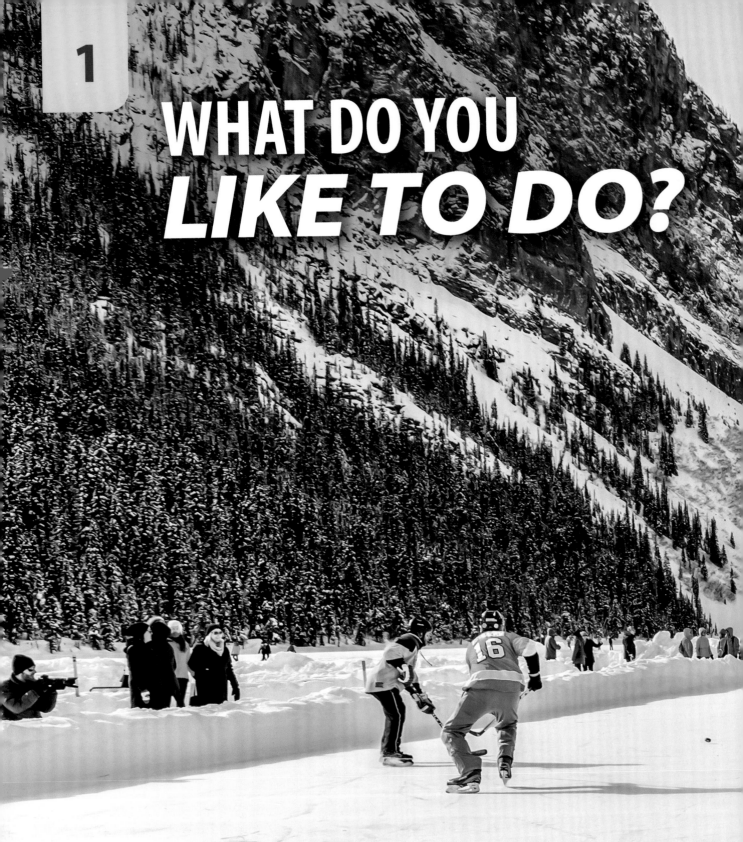

WHAT DO YOU *LIKE TO DO?*

A group of friends
playing in Banff
National Park, Canada

PREVIEW

A **Look at the photo.** What are the people doing?

B **1.1 Listen.** Complete the sentences.

play ice hockey   do origami   collect comic books

play the guitar   draw

1 Sara likes to _____ . She does it twice a week.

2 Daniel likes to _____ . He buys them online.

3 Mari likes to _____ . It's a kind of paper art.

4 Mateo likes to _____ and _____ , but he doesn't like sports.

C **Talk with a partner.** What hobbies do you have?

> What do you like to do?

> I like to draw.

PEOPLE AND PLACES

UNIT GOALS

• describe your hobbies

• use language for describing how often you do something

• learn about what people like to do as hobbies

LANGUAGE FOCUS

A 🎧 1.2 **Listen and read.** What does Stig like to do? Then repeat the conversation and replace the words in **bold**.

Stig: What do you like to do after school, Maya?

Maya: I like to **play video games**. How about you? (**play tennis / draw**)

Stig: Oh, I like to play the **drums**. Hey, I can play for you! (**guitar / piano**)

Maya: Cool!

Maya: Stig, uh, STIG! What else do you like to do?

Stig: Oh! Well, I **like to** sing. What's your favorite song? I can sing it for you. (**love to / often**)

Maya: Um, I'm good. Hey, let's go **play video games**. (**play volleyball / watch TV**)

B 🎧 1.3 **Look at the chart.** Circle the correct answers below.

TALKING ABOUT HOBBIES (USING *LIKE TO* AND EXPRESSIONS OF FREQUENCY)	
What do you like to do after school / on weekends?	**I like to** play music.
Do you like to collect things?	**Yes**, I **do**. / **No**, I **don't**.
How often do you play soccer?	I play **once** / **twice** / **three times** a week. I **never** play soccer.
When do you do karate?	I do it **before** / **after** school on Mondays.

1 When we talk about our hobbies, we say that *I like to* + _____.
   a base verb (e.g., *play*)   **b** simple past (e.g., *played*)

2 *Twice* means _____.
   a one time   **b** two times

3 We use *never* _____ a verb.
   a before   **b** after

C 🎧 1.4 **Listen.** Complete the conversation.

Ming: Nadine, what do you do ¹ _____ school?

Nadine: Well, I play volleyball and I go to
² _____ class.

Ming: Really? ³ _____ play volleyball?

Nadine: I play volleyball ⁴ _____ times a week, Mondays to Wednesdays. My guitar classes are on the other days.

Ming: What do you do before school on weekdays?

Nadine: I play soccer once a week, on ⁵ _____ .

Ming: ⁶ What do you _____ on weekends?

Nadine: I like to do karate on ⁷ _____ . On Sundays, I hang out with my friends!

D **Complete Nadine's schedule.** Use the information in **C.**

Time	Monday	Tuesday	Wednesday	Thursday	Friday	Saturday	Sunday
7:00–8:00							
8:00–3:00			school				
3:00–5:00	volleyball			guitar			

E **Work with a partner.** Complete the **Questions** column of the chart on your own. Then take turns asking your partner questions. Write their answers in the **Answers** column.

Questions	Answers
1 What do you like to do after school?	
2 What do you like to do on weekends?	
3 Do you like to _____ ?	
4 How often do you _____ ?	
5 When do you _____ ?	

BIRDGIRL

Bird expert Mya-Rose Craig likes to travel around the world to see rare birds.

A ▶ 1.1 **Watch the video.** Circle the correct words.

1 Mya-Rose started a **blog / magazine** because she loves birds.

2 Mya-Rose became the **youngest person / first woman** to see 5,000 birds.

3 Nature is important to Mya-Rose—she wants to **open a bird park / save the environment**.

B ▶ 1.1 **Watch again.** Write a number or a word for each answer.

Mya-Rose is [1] _____ years old. She organizes nature [2] _____ for teenagers because she wants them to be interested in the environment. She likes to birdwatch and do [3] _____ activities, such as canoeing. In the future, she wants to be a nature [4] _____ presenter.

C   Read the text. Write the years and phrases to complete the timeline.

Mya-Rose Craig was born in 2002. At the age of nine, she saw her 400th bird. When she was 12, she started her blog, *Birdgirl*. In February 2019, at age 16, she saw her 5,000th bird!

2002 Mya-Rose was born	2011		Mya-Rose saw her 5,000th bird

D   CRITICAL THINKING Applying Talk with a partner. What are some ways to get more people interested in protecting the environment?

PROJECT Do a survey. What kinds of birds are common in your area? Make a list and count the different kinds of birds you see in a day.

PRONUNCIATION reduction: *to*

🎧 1.5 **Listen.** Complete the sentences. Then read the sentences to a partner.

1   What do you _____ ?

2   Do you _____ the piano?

3   I _____ karate.

4   My parents _____ Korean food.

COMMUNICATION

Share your schedule. Student A: Complete the schedule below. Don't show your partner. Ask and answer questions about your partner's schedule. **Student B:** Turn to page 150 and follow the instructions.

Time	Monday	Tuesday	Wednesday	Thursday	Friday
Before school					
Morning					
Lunch					
Afternoon					
After school					

READING

A **Scan the article.** Which of these describe a prodigy? Check (✓) the correct answers.

☐ is young   ☐ has many different interests   ☐ has an amazing skill

B **Skim the article.** Underline some amazing things Alma and Esther did.

C **Talk with a partner.** What kind of prodigy would you like to be?

Alma Deutscher performs at the Burgtheater in Vienna, Austria.

Incredible
TEENS

🎧 1.6 Prodigies are people with **excellent** skills in areas such as art or music. Very often, they are **experts** even before they become teenagers. Fourteen-year-old Alma Deutscher is a music
5 prodigy. She took up piano lessons when she was only two. On her third birthday, she got a violin as a birthday gift. After she tried to play it for a few days, her parents found her a teacher. When she was six, she wrote her first piece of music. Now she
10 performs at concerts around the world.

In many ways, Esther Okade is a typical 14-year-old. In other ways, she is not! She is a math prodigy. She started to learn math when she was three. When she was 10, she started college. She also writes
15 math books for children. Esther's dream is to have her own bank!

Are prodigies born with their skills, or do they just practice a lot? Scientists believe it's both. Prodigies have special **talents**. But they also **practice** a lot to
20 **improve** their skills. Often, their parents have to tell them to **take a break** from their hobbies to eat, sleep, or go to school. Alma, for example, practices and writes music for five hours a day.

Esther Okade studies math in college.

COMPREHENSION

A Answer the questions about *Incredible Teens*.

1 PURPOSE The purpose of this article is to _____ .

   a describe some prodigies' amazing skills

   b explain why prodigies have amazing skills

   c compare different kinds of prodigies

2 INFERENCE Alma's parents got Alma a teacher because _____ .

   a Alma did not like her birthday gift

   b Alma did not know how to play the violin

   c Alma wanted to play the violin instead of the piano

3 DETAIL Esther says she wants to _____ .

   a become rich   b have her own college   c have her own bank

4 REFERENCE In line 21, the word *them* refers to _____ .

   a scientists   b prodigies   c parents

5 DETAIL Which of the following is NOT in the article?

   a Esther's grades in school

   b Esther's age when she started college

   c Alma's age when she took up music lessons

B Complete the notes. Choose one word from the article for each answer.

Prodigies	
• have special talents	
• [1] _____ a lot	

Alma Deutscher	**Esther Okade**
• wrote her first piece of music at the age of [2] _____	• started learning math at the age of [4] _____
• practices and writes music for [3] _____ hours a day	• started [5] _____ at the age of 10

C CRITICAL THINKING Justifying **Talk with a partner.** Is it good or bad for child prodigies to start college at a young age?

VOCABULARY

A **Find the words below in the article.** Then circle the correct answers.

1 Someone with **excellent** skills in math is **good** / **bad** at it.

2 An **expert** knows **a lot** / **very little** about something.

3 A **talent** is a skill that someone **gets by doing many times** / **is born with**.

4 When you **practice**, you do something **once** / **many times**.

5 When you **improve** at a skill, you become **better** / **worse** at it.

6 When you **take a break** from something, you **start** / **stop** doing it.

B **Read the information below.** Then complete the sentences using *apart*, *back*, *out*, or *up*.

> Phrasal verbs with *take* have different meanings.
>
> *take* something *apart*: remove parts of something
>
> *take* something *back*: return
>
> *take* someone *out*: go to a place with someone and pay for them
>
> *take up*: start something new (hobby, lessons, etc.)

1 She took _____ ice hockey when she was six.

2 The dress is too big for Lucia. She wants to take it _____ to the store.

3 Si Woo's parents took him _____ for dinner.

4 The boy is taking his toy robot _____ .

DO YOU KNOW?

Bob Bretall has about _____ comic books in his collection.
a 1,000
b 10,000
c 100,000

WRITING

A **Read the email.**

B **Think about some of your hobbies.** How often do you do them?

C **Write an email to a new friend.** Write about your hobbies and invite your friend to one of them.

New message

To **Sophia**

Subject **How are you?**

Hi Sophia,

How are you? What do you like to do after school? I like to go running. I'm in a running club. Do you want to come running with us? We meet three times a week on …

Best wishes,
Amy

Send

TEEN *ROCK CLIMBER*

Before You Watch

Talk with a partner. Look at the photo. What skills do you need to have to be good at rock climbing?

While You Watch

A ▶ 1.2 **Watch the video.** Circle the correct answers.

1 When Kai competed at his first world championship, he came in **first** / **fourth**.

2 Kai **often** / **rarely** hangs out with his friends after school.

3 The Triangle Rock Club is about **30** / **90** minutes away from his home.

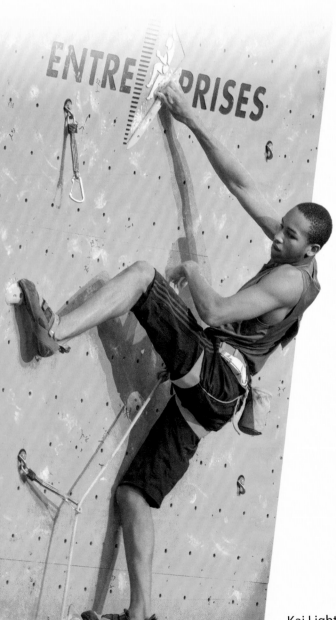

B ▶ 1.2 **Watch again.** Circle **T** for True or **F** for False.

Kai Lightner …

1 has a rock climbing coach.

   T   **F**

2 climbs before he goes to school.

   T   **F**

3 comes from a city where rock climbing is popular.

   T   **F**

4 thinks that climbing outdoors is more difficult than climbing indoors.

   T   **F**

C Circle the correct answer.
What does *discipline* mean?

a to give up

b to think of new ways to do something

c to keep working on something that is difficult

After You Watch

Talk with a partner. Why do you think students like Kai are able to do well in school and activities outside of school?

Kai Lightner competes in a rock climbing competition.

A Complete the words.

1 A kind of paper art   _o_ ___ ___ ___ ___ ___ _i_

2 Make something better
    _i_ ___ _m_ ___ ___ ___ ___ _e_ ___

3 Something that a person likes to do
    _h_ ___ ___ _b_ ___ ___ _y_ ___

4 Describes something that's very good
    _e_ ___ ___ ___ ___ _l_ ___ ___ ___ _t_ ___

5 Something that prodigies do to get better at their skills
    _p_ ___ ___ ___ _t_ ___ ___ _e_ ___

B Complete the conversation. Use the words to write sentences.

Kylie: What do you like to do?

Lucas: (play the guitar) [1] _I like to play the guitar._

Kylie: (how often / play the guitar)
    [2] _____ ?

Lucas: (twice a week) [3] _____ .

Kylie: (when / play the guitar) [4] _____ ?

Lucas: I play it after school.

C Complete the sentences using *apart*, *back*, *out*, or *up*.

1 Rika took Sofia _____ for lunch.

2 An engineer took the machine _____ .

3 Thanh's new computer wasn't working so she took it _____
to the store.

4 I was eight when I took _____ the piano.

SELF CHECK   Now I can …

☐ describe my hobbies

☐ use language for describing how often I do something

☐ talk about what people like to do as hobbies

2

WHAT DOES *SHE* LOOK LIKE?

PREVIEW

A 🎧 **2.1** **Listen.** Circle the words you hear.

1 Person A has **short** / shoulder-length white hair.   2

2 Person B has **spiky** / **curly** black hair.   ___

3 Person C has long **straight** / **wavy** blond hair.   ___

4 Person D has **red** / **black** hair and a **beard** / **mustache**.   ___

5 Person E has **short** / **long** blond hair. She wears glasses, too.   ___

2

3

4 SHORT BLACK HAIR, BLUE EYES

6

7 STRAIGHT BROWN HAIR

8

10

11 LONG RED HAIR

12

Look at the photos (1–12). Match the photos with the descriptions in **A**.

Work with a partner. Choose three people in the photos and describe them to your partner. Your partner guesses the people.

UNIT GOALS

- ask about a person's physical appearance
- use language for describing a person's physical appearance
- learn about some people with interesting facial hair

LANGUAGE FOCUS

A 🎧 2.2 **Listen and read.** What does Emily look like? Then repeat the conversation and replace the words in **bold**.

REAL ENGLISH I'm on my way.

Nadine:	Ming, I'm at the **concert** now. Where are you? (**soccer game / rugby match**)
Ming:	Sorry, I'm late. I'm on my way. Do you see Emily?
Nadine:	Emily? What does she look like?
Ming:	She's **tall** and slim. (**short / medium height**)
Nadine:	OK … Oh! Does she have **short blond** hair? (**long black / curly red**)
Ming:	Yeah, and she has **blue** eyes. (**brown / green**)
Nadine:	I see her! **Excuse me**, are you Emily? I'm … Oh! Stig, it's you! (**Hello / Hi there**)

B 🎧 2.3 **Look at the chart.** Circle the correct answers below.

DESCRIBING PEOPLE (USING DESCRIPTIVE ADJECTIVES)	
What does he **look like?**	He**'s tall** and he **has** short curly **hair**. He**'s medium height** and he **has** a **beard**.
What do you **look like?**	I**'m short** and I **have** brown **eyes**. I **have freckles** and I **wear glasses**. I**'m slim** and I **wear braces**.

1 We use *wears* / *is* to talk about someone's height.

2 We use *is* / *has* to talk about someone's hair and eye color.

3 We use *is* / *wears* to talk about someone's glasses or things they put on and take off.

4 We use *has* / *wears* to talk about someone's freckles, beard, or mustache.

C 🎧 2.4 **Complete the conversations.** Then listen and check your answers.

1 **A:** Hey, there's a new boy in class.

   B: Oh, really? What ¹ _____ ?

   A: He ² _____ tall and he ³ _____ blond hair.

2 **A:** Do you see my sisters?

   B: ⁴ _____ look like?

   A: They ⁵ _____ glasses and they ⁶ _____ short black hair.

D **Look at the photo below.** Complete the sentences.

glasses	brown	tall	blond	curly

1 He has short _____ hair. He wears _____ , too.

2 He's _____ and he has short hair.

3 She has _____ black hair.

4 She has straight _____ hair.

E **Work with a partner. Student A:** Choose a famous person. Describe them to your partner.
Student B: Guess the famous person.

This person is an actress. She's tall. She has long blond hair. She has blue eyes.

Is it Jennifer Lawrence?

NEVER FORGET
A FACE

People use a facial recognition system to pay for things in Wenzhou, China.

A ▶ 2.1 **Watch Part 1 of the video.** Circle **T** for True or **F** for False.

1   Eric has short blond hair.   T   F

2   Eric wears glasses.   T   F

3   Eric has brown eyes.   T   F

4   Eric has freckles.   T   F

B ▶ 2.2 **Watch Part 2 of the video.** Which parts of Eric's face did you remember correctly? Compare your results with a partner.

C **Complete the paragraph below.** Use the words in the box.

> brain   difficult   part   nose   face   whole

To most people, it's a [1] _____ task to remember a person's face. This is because the [2] _____ sees a face as a puzzle. One part of the brain recognizes the different parts of a [3] _____ , such as the eyes, [4] _____ , and mouth. Another part of the brain puts these different parts together to recognize them as someone's face. So it's easier to remember a face as a [5] _____ rather than each different [6] _____ .

D `CRITICAL THINKING Evaluating` **Talk with a partner.** What do you know about computer facial recognition? Do you think it's a good thing or a bad thing?

> **PROJECT Student A:** Show a photo of someone you know to your partner. After 60 seconds, put the photo away. **Student B:** Describe the face of the person in the photo. Then compare Student B's description with the photo. How different are they?

PRONUNCIATION consonant blends: *bl, br, gl, gr*

A 🎧 2.5 **Listen.** Circle the sounds you hear.

1 gr	br	**2** gl	bl	**3** gl	bl	**4** br	gr
5 bl	gl	**6** gr	br	**7** gr	br	**8** gr	br

B **Work with a partner.** Take turns reading the words below.

1 braces	**2** grow	**3** glad	**4** blink
5 bring	**6** blow	**7** global	**8** greet

COMMUNICATION

Work with a partner. Look at the photos on page 150. **Student A:** Choose one person in the photos. Don't tell your partner who it is. **Student B:** Ask yes/no questions to guess your partner's choice. Take turns.

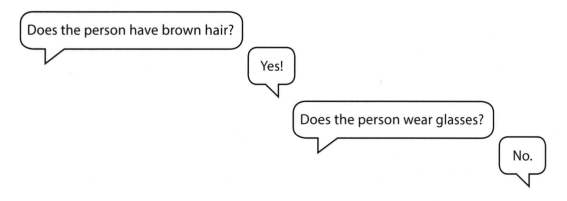

Does the person have brown hair?

Yes!

Does the person wear glasses?

No.

READING

A **Look at the photos.** What's surprising about the famous people in them?

B **Scan the article.** Madame Tussaud was a _____.

  a teacher   **b** hair stylist   **c** nurse

C **Scan the article.** How long does it take to make a wax statue?

An artist paints a statue's face at a Madame Tussauds museum.

THE WORLD OF
MADAME TUSSAUDS

🎧 **2.6** You can **touch** these famous people as much as you want. And they **don't mind**—they're made of wax! At Madame Tussauds museums, visitors can see **lifelike** wax statues of famous
5 people. There are over 20 of these museums around the world.

Madame Marie Tussaud started the first Madame Tussauds museum over 200 years ago. She was an art teacher in France. She made wax masks of
10 important people such as King Louis XVI.

An artist takes about four months to make each wax statue. First, they take photographs of the person. They use these to **create** the shape of the wax statue. It takes a lot of wax to make a statue—the
15 head **alone** uses about 5 kilograms of wax! Next, the artists add human hair onto the heads. It takes about 140 hours to finish a statue's hair! They then paint the faces. They use over 20 colors for the skin and teeth. Finally, stylists dress the statues.

20 Museum **staff** checks each statue every day. They often change the clothes and wash the statues' hair. Sometimes, a statue's hairstyle changes, too!

A stylist combs a statue's hair.

COMPREHENSION

A **Answer the questions about *The World of Madame Tussauds.***

IDIOM

"I couldn't keep a straight face" means I _____.
a cried
b laughed
c talked

1 **MAIN IDEA** The article is mainly about _____.

   a how wax statues are made

   b how Madame Tussaud started her wax museum

   c how popular these wax museums are

2 **INFERENCE** Madame Tussauds museum is LEAST likely to have a statue of _____.

   a a singer   b a teacher   c a sports star

3 **PURPOSE** Why does the author mention the number of Madame Tussauds museums around the world?

   a to show how the museums are different around the world

   b to show that each museum has many statues

   c to show how popular the museums are

4 **REFERENCE** In line 12, the word *they* refers to the _____.

   a statues   b artists   c museum visitors

5 **DETAIL** Which of the following is NOT in the article?

   a the cost of a wax statue

   b the time it takes to finish a statue's hair

   c the amount of wax needed to make a statue's head

B **Complete the chart.** What are the steps to make a wax statue? Use one word from the article for each answer.

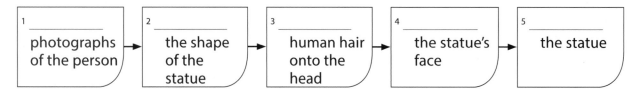

1 _____ photographs of the person → 2 _____ the shape of the statue → 3 _____ human hair onto the head → 4 _____ the statue's face → 5 _____ the statue

C **CRITICAL THINKING** **Personalizing** **Talk with a partner.** Imagine you are starting a wax museum. Which wax figures would you like to include?

VOCABULARY

A Find the words below in the article. Then complete the sentences using the words in the box.

touch	don't mind	lifelike	create	alone	staff

1 The _____ at the museum is friendly.

2 The artists love to _____ beautiful wax statues.

3 If you do something _____, you do it without other people.

4 You cannot _____ the statues in some museums.

5 Visitors to the museum _____ that the place is noisy.

6 The statue of the horse is so _____—even its eyes look real.

B Read the information below. Then complete the sentences with the correct form of *feel*, *look*, *smell*, *sound*, or *taste*.

> *Feel*, *look*, *smell*, *sound*, and *taste* are sense verbs. We can use **sense verb** + *like* + **noun** to describe things.

1 The wax statues at Madame Tussauds museums _____ like people.

2 The soap _____ like flowers.

3 The science museum is so noisy—it _____ like a children's playground.

4 This drink looks like water but it _____ like soda.

5 His skin is so soft—it _____ like a baby's skin.

WRITING

A Read the paragraph.

B Write a description of your physical appearance. Don't write your name.

C Make a guess. Shuffle your paragraph together with your classmates'. Choose one and read it. Then try to find the person.

I'm tall and slim. I wear glasses. I have long black hair and brown eyes.

GREAT FACIAL HAIR

Before You Watch

Look at the pictures below. Guess the names of the facial hair styles.

pencil   musketeer   Dali   goatee   full beard

_____   _____   _____   _____   _____

While You Watch

A ▶ 2.3 **Watch the video.** Check (✓) the mustaches and beards above that you see.

B ▶ 2.3 **Watch again.** Circle the correct answers.

1 The competition takes place every **year** / **two years**.

2 John has a **brown** / **white** beard.

3 Leo has a long, **curly** / **straight** black mustache.

4 Jack Passion won the competition with his
   short brown / **long red** beard.

C **Match.** Join the names to the descriptions.

1 John   ○   ○   wrote a book about his beard.

2 Leo   ○   ○   won second place for the Brown Bear category.

3 Jack   ○   ○   travels around the world to join competitions.

After You Watch

Talk with a partner. Does anyone in your family have a beard
or mustache? What's it like? Why do you think some people
want to grow a beard or a mustache?

A contestant shows off his beard at the
World Beard and Mustache Championships.

A Complete the sentences. Circle the correct answers.

New message	_ □ ×
To	Horaz
Subject	Hello!

Hi Horaz,

Thank you for your email.

I made some really good friends here. My best friend is Karen. She's medium [1] **height / short / tall**. She has long blond hair and blue eyes. Like me, she wears [2] **glasses / slim / freckles**. She has a talent for drawing. Her drawings of people are very [3] **lifelike / spiky / wavy**. She also [4] **touched / created / played** posters for our school concert. If you come to visit us, she can draw a picture of you. Hope to see you soon!

Your cousin,
Zoe

B Complete the conversation.

A: What does she [1] _____ like?

B: She [2] _____ average height and she [3] _____ blue eyes.

A: Does she [4] _____ glasses?

B: Yes, she does.

C Match. Join the phrases to the words.

1 There are so many people in this room—it sounds like ○   ○ a bakery.

2 It's so warm in this room—it feels like ○   ○ a party.

3 This house is so big—it looks like ○   ○ an oven.

4 The burger is terrible—it tastes like ○   ○ a castle.

5 She just made bread, so the kitchen smells like ○   ○ cardboard.

SELF CHECK   Now I can …

☐ ask about a person's physical appearance

☐ use language for describing physical appearance

☐ describe people with interesting facial hair

WHEN DID YOU BUY
THAT SHIRT?

Shoppers take a break from shopping in Florence, Italy.

PREVIEW

A 🎧 **3.1** **Listen.** Number the items.

watch _____   T-shirt _____   jacket __1__

sweater _____   skirt _____   shoes _____

glasses _____   pants _____

B **Group the clothing items in A.**

Tops: _____

Bottoms: _____

Footwear: _____

Accessories: _____

C **Talk with a partner.** Look at the photo. What are the people wearing? What do you like to wear?

> What kind of clothes do you like to wear?

> I like to wear a T-shirt, jeans, and a hat.

HISTORY AND CULTURE

UNIT GOALS

• describe when you did something

• use language for talking about clothes

• learn why the color of your outfit is important

LANGUAGE FOCUS

A 🎧 **3.2 Listen and read.** What clothes did Maya wear? Then repeat the conversation and replace the words in **bold**.

> **REAL ENGLISH** What's wrong?

Nadine: Are you ready, Maya?

Maya: No! I don't have anything to wear to the **dance**. (**party / picnic**)

Nadine: But you just went shopping **last week**. (**two days ago / on Saturday**)

Maya: Yeah, and I bought a nice **black skirt**. (**pair of pants / pair of jeans**)

Nadine: OK, great. Do you have a top?

Maya: Yes, my mom gave me a new top **a few days ago**. But … (**yesterday / last night**)

Nadine: **What's wrong**? (**What's the problem / What's the matter**)

Maya: We're wearing the same outfit!

B 🎧 **3.3 Look at the chart.** Complete the sentences below with *last*, *ago*, or *just*.

TALKING ABOUT SHOPPING (USING TIME ADVERBIALS)			
I like your sweater. Did you get it **recently**?	Yes, I bought it	**last**	weekend. night. week.
When did you buy your dress?	I bought it	a week	**ago**.
Are those new sneakers?	Yes, I **just** bought them	two days	**ago**.
	No, I got them	a couple of months a year	

1 We use length of time (e.g., *two weeks*) + _____ to refer to a specific time period in the past.

2 We use _____ + time word to talk about the time period most recent or closest to now.

3 We use _____ + verb to talk about something that happened very recently.

C 🎧 **3.4** **Complete the conversation.** Write the correct form of the verbs or time expressions with *last*, *ago*, *just*, or *recently*. Then listen and check your answers.

Paula: Dad, I need new clothes for school.

Dad: But you already have so many. What about that blue dress? Didn't you get that ¹ _____ ?

Paula: Dad, I ² _____ (**buy**) that dress
³ _____ (**two years**). It's too small now.

Dad: Oh, okay. Then how about your green top?

Paula: Mom ⁴ _____ (**give**) it to me ⁵ _____ (**summer**), but
I ⁶ _____ tore it ⁷ _____ (**night**)!

Dad: All right, all right. Let's go shopping this weekend.

D **Complete the sentences.** Put the words in the correct order to make sentences.

1 did / you / shirt / when / your / buy

_____?

2 weekend / bought / dress / green / Zoe / a / last

_____.

3 black / recently / Kei / buy / did / his / shirt

_____?

4 two months / Yun / new / skirt / ago / a / got

_____.

E **Work in a group.** Play a chain game. Name the last item of clothing or accessory you bought and when you bought it. Your group members continue the chain.

I bought a pair of sneakers last weekend.

Jun bought a pair of sneakers last weekend. I got a red shirt recently.

THE REAL WORLD

CLOTHING COLORS

The color of your clothes affects how others see you.

A **Look at the photo.** Make a list of the colors you see. How does each color make you feel?

B ▶ 3.1 **Watch Part 1 of the video.** Match to complete the sentences.

1 In red, Coren seems ○   ○ interesting.

2 In black, Coren looks ○   ○ helpful.

3 In blue, Coren seems more ○ ○ powerful.

C ▶ 3.2 **Predict.** What color should you wear? Then watch **Part 2** of the video and check your answers.

1 Wear **red** / **blue** clothes for a night out.

2 For a business meeting, wear something **red** / **black**.

3 To make new friends, wear **black** / **blue** clothes.

D 🎧 3.5 (CRITICAL THINKING Applying) **Complete the sentences using the words in the box. Then listen and check your ideas.**

gray	white	green	orange	brown

1 _____ is the color of the earth. A person wearing this color seems honest.

2 Scientists say that the color _____ gives a feeling of peace.

3 _____ is not bright or dark. Most people in this color do not like attention.

4 Fun and happy people like to wear the color _____ .

5 Neat people like to wear the color _____ .

PROJECT Make a chart. Record your friends' and family's clothing for a week. Do you think their color choices show what type of person they are? Share with the class.

PRONUNCIATION consonant blends with *s: sm, sn, sw, sk, sl, st*

A 🎧 3.6 **Listen.** Circle the sounds you hear.

1 sk   sm   2 sl   sm   3 sn   st   4 sn   sk   5 st   sl   6 sw   sk

B **Work with a partner.** Take turns reading the words below.

1 small   2 sneakers   3 sweater   4 skirt   5 sleeve   6 style

COMMUNICATION

Do a survey. For each item, find someone who wore it recently. Write the name of the person and ask when he or she wore it.

Item	Who?	When?	Item	Who?	When?
a hat			a shirt		
a watch			a skirt		
a dress			pants		
jeans			a sweater		
socks			sneakers		

Did you wear a hat recently?

Yes, I did. I wore one two days ago.

READING

A Look at the title and the photo. What do you think a yarn bomb is? Check (✓) the correct answers.

- ☐ a kind of street art
- ☐ a dangerous object
- ☐ a type of clothing

B Scan the article. In which city did London Kaye knit a huge sign?

C Talk with a partner. Why do you think people like to yarn bomb?

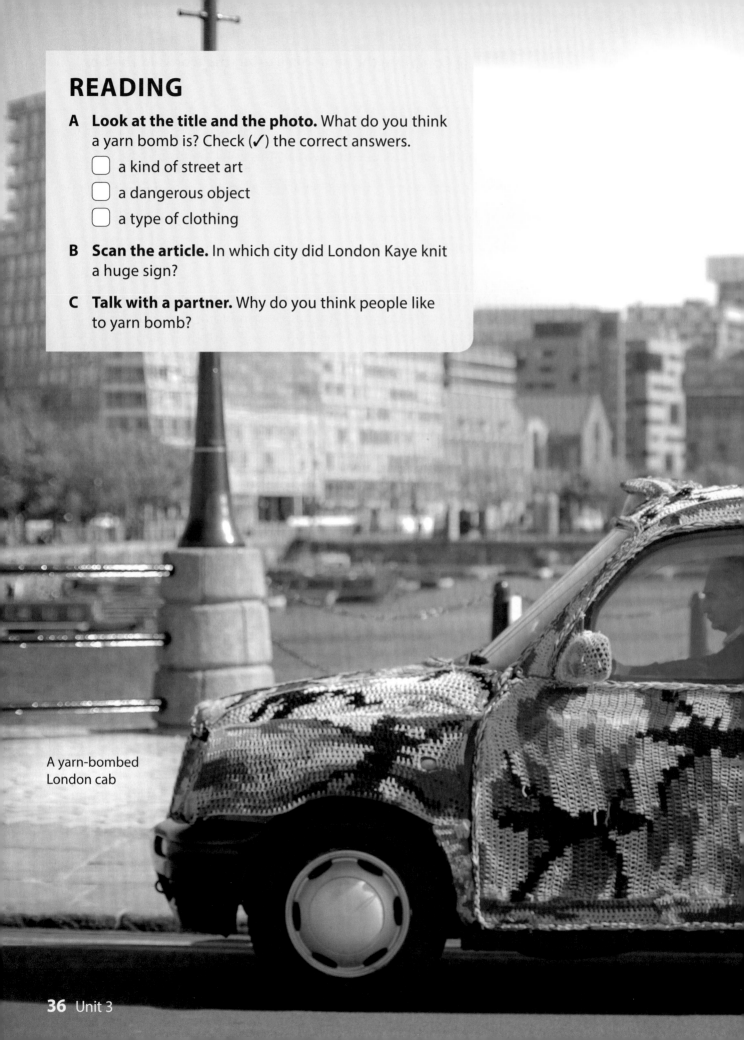

A yarn-bombed London cab

YARN BOMB!

A 🎧 **3.7** Some people knit yarn to make clothes, and some people yarn bomb! Yarn bombing is a kind of street art. People knit colorful "coats" to cover large things, such as cars, trees, and even **whole** buildings!

B London Kaye is an artist and yarn bomber from Los Angeles, California. More than four years ago, she was working at a computer store. She sold a computer to Olek, a famous yarn artist. Olek was carrying a bag that she knitted. London saw Olek's bag and wanted to learn more. This was how she first **discovered** yarn bombing.

C First, London made a colorful scarf and **wrapped** it around a tree. She thought someone would take it down, but nobody did. So she had an idea: yarn bomb a new thing every day for 30 days **in a row**. She made it: in fact, she reached 50! Her work quickly got attention. Starbucks paid her to yarn bomb one of its new stores. She even knitted a big sign in Times Square in New York City.

D Yarn bombing is becoming popular around the world. You can find yarn bombing in many cities, such as Paris and Mexico City. You can also find it in **rural** areas. Yarn bombers tell stories through their art. They want to make their **environment** more colorful and interesting. They also want people to see their cities differently.

COMPREHENSION

A Answer the questions about *Yarn Bomb!*

1 `DETAIL` Which of the following do yarn bombers NOT cover with a knitted "jacket"?

   a cars　　　　　　　　**b** people　　　　　　　**c** buildings

2 `DETAIL` London was _____ before she started yarn bombing.

   a an artist　　　　　　**b** an engineer　　　　　**c** a salesperson

3 `INFERENCE` From the article, we can infer that Olek's bag was _____.

   a beautiful　　　　　　**b** big　　　　　　　　**c** useful

4 `REFERENCE` The word *it* in the second sentence of paragraph C refers to _____.

   a the tree　　　　　　　**b** the scarf　　　　　　**c** the computer store

5 `MAIN IDEA` Paragraph D is mainly about _____.

   a famous yarn bombs around the world

   b why people yarn bomb

   c the future of yarn bombing

B Complete the chart. Write notes about yarn bombing.

What is yarn bombing?	Where does it take place?	Why do people do it?

C `CRITICAL THINKING  Evaluating` Talk with a partner. Yarn bombers think that their art makes the environment more interesting. Do you agree? Can you think of any problems with yarn bombing?

London Kaye works in her studio in Brooklyn, New York City.

VOCABULARY

A Find the words below in the article. Then circle the correct answers.

1 A **whole** building is **all** / **some** of its parts.

2 When you **discover** something, **you find out** / **don't care** about it.

3 When you **wrap** something, you **cover it** / **leave it open**.

4 Thirty days **in a row** is the same as **once a month** / **every day for a month**.

5 A **rural** area is **close to** / **far outside** a city.

6 An animal's **environment** is **where it lives** / **what it looks like**.

B Read the information below. Then circle the correct answers.

> Phrasal verbs about clothes
>
> *put on:* wear
>
> *take off:* remove
>
> *try on:* put on a piece of clothing to see how it looks and if it fits

1 **Try on** / **Take off** your shoes before you go into the house.

2 **Put on** / **Try on** your gloves—it's cold outside.

3 That's a nice jacket. **Take it off!** / **Try it on!**

 **Anna Davis**
@anna_davis

This outfit has a white top, a pink sweater, and a pair of jeans. I like this outfit because it looks comfortable and …

WRITING

A Look at the social media post. Read the beginning of the description of the outfit.

B Find a photograph of an outfit you like.

C Write a social media post. Describe the outfit and explain why you like it.

THE **THIRSTY COTTON T-SHIRT**

Before You Watch

Talk with a partner. How often do you wear T-shirts? How many T-shirts do you have? When did you last buy a T-shirt?

While You Watch

A ▶ 3.3 **Watch the video.** Which of the following uses the most energy?

a   growing cotton plants   b   making clothes   c   washing and drying
                                   from cotton   cotton clothes

B ▶ 3.3 **Watch again.** Circle **T** for True or **F** for False.

1   The amount of water used to make one T-shirt is more than a
    person drinks in two years.   T   F

2   We use five times more energy to wash clothes than to dry them.   T   F

3   About 2% of the water on Earth is salty.   T   F

4   About 7% of the water we use goes into growing crops.   T   F

C   Talk with a partner. For the false sentence(s), say the true information.

After You Watch

Talk with a partner. How often do you
wash and iron your clothes? What can
you do to use less water and energy?

Cotton comes from
cotton plants.

A Complete the sentences. Use the words in the box.

> rural   glasses   wrap   T-shirt   in a row   watches

1 She wears her _____ to see the words on the board.

2 _____ a scarf around your neck if you are cold.

3 I wore red shoes three days _____ last week.

4 This _____ area has many farms.

5 How much water do we use to make a cotton _____ ?

6 This shop sells accessories such as hats and _____ .

B Complete the sentences. Circle the correct answers.

1 I got these shoes **last** / **ago** weekend.

2 She got new glasses three days **just** / **ago**.

3 I **last** / **just** bought these sneakers yesterday.

4 Did you get a blue skirt **just** / **recently**?

5 He wore his new jacket to the party **last** / **just** night.

C Complete the sentences using *off* **or** *on.*

1 Every morning, I take _____ my pajamas.

2 On cold days, I put _____ a sweater.

3 I often try _____ clothes before I buy them.

SELF CHECK   Now I can …

☐ describe when I did something

☐ use language for talking about clothes

☐ talk about why the color of my outfit is important

WHAT'S THE COLDEST PLACE ON EARTH?

PREVIEW

A **Look at the questions below.** Discuss your answers with a partner.

1   What's the largest desert on Earth?

   a The Gobi   **b** The Sahara

2   What's the highest waterfall in the world?

   a Angel Falls   **b** Niagara Falls

3   Where's the smallest hotel in the world?

   a Thailand   **b** Germany

4   What's the biggest rock on Earth?

   a Uluru/Ayers Rock   **b** Zuma Rock

5   Where's the coldest place on Earth?

   a The Arctic   **b** Antarctica

6   Where's the tallest tree in the world?

   a The United States   **b** Mexico

7   What's the smallest country in the world?

   a Vatican City   **b** The Maldives

B   🎧 4.1   **Listen.** Circle the correct answers in **A**.

C **Talk with a partner.** What do you know about the places and things in **A**?

> The Sahara is in Africa.

THE NATURAL WORLD

UNIT GOALS

• compare three or more things

• learn language for describing extreme places and things

• talk about the Amazon

A mountaineer stands in front of a mountain range on Livingston Island, Antarctica.

LANGUAGE FOCUS

A 🎧 4.2 **Listen and read.** What test is Nadine studying for? Then repeat the conversation and replace the words in **bold**.

REAL ENGLISH Let's see.

Ming: Hey, Nadine! Do you want to watch a movie after school?

Nadine: I can't. I have a **geography** test. (**science / social studies**) It's my **most difficult** subject. (**toughest / most challenging**)

Ming: Let me help! Let's see. What's the **coldest continent** in the world? (**biggest insect / oldest culture**)

Nadine: Oh, that's easy! Everyone knows that!

Ming: OK, so what's the world's **highest mountain**? (**most dangerous plant / most common language**)

Nadine: Well, that's easy, too!

Ming: Okay. Then what are you worried about?

Nadine: Because my test is tomorrow, and I have the world's shortest memory!

B 🎧 4.3 **Look at the chart.** Circle the correct answers below.

DESCRIBING EXTREMES (USING SUPERLATIVES)				
What's **the largest** beetle in the world?	The titan beetle is **the largest** beetle.	big	→	the bi**gg**est
		pretty	→	the prett**i**est
What's **the tiniest** dog in the world?	**The tiniest** dog is the Chihuahua.	famous	→	the **most** famous
		good	→	the **best**
Some people think that Komodo Beach in Indonesia has **the most beautiful** sand in the world.		bad	→	the **worst**
		less	→	the **least**

1 We use superlatives when talking about **two / three or more** things.

2 Superlatives go **before / after** the nouns they're describing.

3 For adjectives with three or more syllables (e.g., *interesting*), we **use *the most* + adjective / add *-est* to the adjective**.

C Complete the sentences. Use the correct form of the words in parentheses.

1 Lake Baikal in Russia is _____ (**deep**) lake in the world.

2 Some of _____ (**bad**) storms in the world happen in India.

3 Some people think that Atenas, Costa Rica, has _____ (**good**) weather in the world.

4 Many people say that Paris is _____ (**beautiful**) city in the world.

5 The _____ (**less expensive**) way to travel from London to Paris is by bus.

6 Soccer is _____ (**popular**) sport in the world.

D 🎧 4.4 **Complete the sentences.** Use the correct form of the words in the box. Then listen and check your answers.

small	fast	dangerous	heavy

1 The blue whale is _____ animal in the world.

2 The inland taipan is one of _____ snakes in the world.

3 The falcon is _____ bird in the world.

4 The pygmy marmoset is _____ monkey in the world.

E Work with a partner. Use the words in the box to talk about things you know about.

most	least	long	short	high	low
big	small	hot	cold	dry	wet

The highest mountain in my country is Mount Fuji.

February is the coldest month in my city.

GOING TO
EXTREMES

The only shop in Oymyakon

A **Read the information about Nick Middleton.** What are his jobs?

Explorer Nick Middleton teaches at Oxford University in England. In an interview with National Geographic Learning, he talks about his trip to the world's coldest town: Oymyakon, in Siberia, Russia.

a explorer and artist   b writer and photographer   c teacher and explorer

B ▶ 4.1 **Watch the video.** What do people usually eat or drink in Oymyakon? Check (✓) three correct answers.

☐ reindeer   ☐ fruits   ☐ rice

☐ horse   ☐ milk   ☐ vegetables

C ▶ 4.1 **Watch again.** Circle **T** for True or **F** for False.

1 Vegetables grow all year in Oymyakon.   **T**   **F**

2 To keep warm, people in Oymyakon wear clothes made of reindeer fur.   **T**   **F**

3 People in Oymyakon sometimes sell animals to make money.   **T**   **F**

D **CRITICAL THINKING** **Justifying** **Talk with a partner.** What do you think is the most difficult thing about living in Oymyakon? Give reasons for your answer.

PROJECT Make a list. Imagine you are going to an extreme place for three days. Choose a type of place (hot, dry desert or freezing, icy mountain, etc.). Make a list of the 10 most important things you need to survive there.

PRONUNCIATION sentence stress

🎧 4.5 **Listen.** Underline the stressed words. Take turns reading the sentence.

1 <u>Antarctica</u> is the <u>coldest place</u> on <u>Earth</u>.

2 What's the most famous city in Europe?

3 New York City is the largest city in the world by area.

4 The Congo River is the deepest river in the world.

5 Where's the tallest waterfall in South America?

6 The Amazon is the largest river in the world.

COMMUNICATION

Play a quiz game. Work with a partner. **Student A:** Turn to page 151. **Student B:** Turn to page 152. Take turns asking and answering questions.

A village in Greenland

READING

A **Scan the article.** Where does the Amazon River begin and end?

B **Skim the article.** Find two examples of why the Amazon is extreme.

C **Talk with a partner.** Do you think the Amazon is important to us? Why?

EXTREME AMAZON!

🎧 4.6 Twenty percent of all the water that goes into the world's oceans comes from one river—the Amazon.

The Amazon River begins in the Andes Mountains in
5 Peru. It travels more than 6,000 kilometers to the Atlantic Ocean. Most of the Amazon's water comes from rain. During the wet season, parts of the river are 190 kilometers wide.

More than half of the Amazon River is in Brazil. Here,
10 it **flows** through the world's largest rainforest. The Amazon rainforest has the largest number of plant and animal **species** on Earth. It has about 40,000 plant species and 3,000 kinds of fish. It also has 1,300 types of birds and over 2 million species
15 of **insects**!

Some of the Amazon's animals are dangerous. The anaconda is one of the world's largest snakes. It's also one of the scariest animals in the Amazon. But there are also **gentle** animals, like the sloth and the
20 pink dolphin.

The Amazon is very important to our **planet**. There are still many kinds of animals and plants for us to discover. If we lose the Amazon, we'll **lose** a big part of life on Earth.

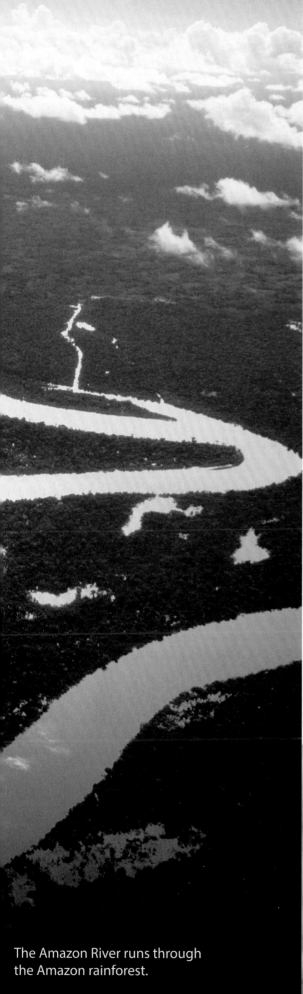

The Amazon River runs through the Amazon rainforest.

A pale-throated sloth in Manaus, Brazil

COMPREHENSION

A Answer the questions about *Extreme Amazon!*

1 **MAIN IDEA** The article is mainly about the Amazon's _____ .

   a people   **b** weather   **c** importance

2 **INFERENCE** The Amazon River is narrower during the _____ season.

   a dry   **b** cold   **c** rainy

3 **REFERENCE** The word *Here* in line 9 refers to _____ .

   a the Atlantic Ocean   **b** Peru   **c** Brazil

4 **DETAIL** Which group of animals has the greatest number of species in the Amazon?

   a fish   **b** insects   **c** birds

5 **DETAIL** Which of the following is NOT a gentle animal?

   a anaconda   **b** sloth   **c** pink dolphin

B Complete the word web. Use one word from the article for each answer.

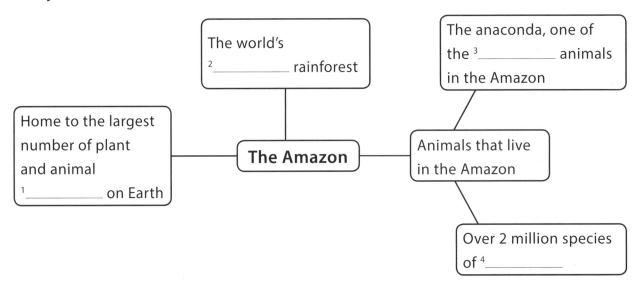

C **CRITICAL THINKING Analyzing** **Talk with a partner.** Read the sentences below. Determine if each sentence is a fact or an opinion. Circle the correct answers.

1 Most of the Amazon's water comes from rain.   **Fact   Opinion**

2 The Amazon is the world's largest rainforest.   **Fact   Opinion**

3 There are interesting plants and animals in   **Fact   Opinion**
  the Amazon.

4 The anaconda is one of the scariest animals   **Fact   Opinion**
  in the Amazon.

VOCABULARY

A Find the words below in the article. Then complete the sentences using the words in the box.

IDIOM

To "go to extremes" means to _____.
a do more than is necessary
b visit an extreme place

flows	species	insect	gentle	planet	lose

1 The water _____ down the mountain and into the sea.

2 The turtle is a quiet, _____ animal.

3 When there is a forest fire, we _____ many trees.

4 There are many _____ of birds in the Amazon.

5 The ant is a(n) _____ .

6 Earth is a(n) _____ .

B Read the information below. Then match the words to the numbers.

> We can write numbers in words.
>
>   1 *thousand* = 1,000   1 *million* = 1,000,000   1 *billion* = 1,000,000,000
>
> To describe numbers that are less than 1, we use *fractions*, e.g., ½ (half), or *decimals*, 0.5 (zero point five).

1 one million	○	○	10.5
2 ten thousand	○	○	10,000,000,000
3 ten billion	○	○	½
4 half	○	○	1,500
5 one thousand five hundred	○	○	10,000
6 ten point five	○	○	1,000,000

SWITZERLAND is a great place to visit. It has the Matterhorn, which is one of the most beautiful mountains in the world . . .

WRITING

A Look at the poster. Read the beginning of the description of the photo.

B Choose a great travel destination. Find a photo of it. Make notes about it.

C Make a poster. Describe the place. Explain what makes it special. Use your notes from **B**.

ICY ANTARCTICA

Before You Watch

Talk with a partner. What words can you use to describe Antarctica? How is it different from your country?

While You Watch

A   ▶ 4.2 **Watch the video.** Which of these statements about Antarctica is NOT true? Circle the correct answer.

   a It has a winter and a summer.

   b It's closed to tourists.

   c It gets very little rain.

B   ▶ 4.2 **Watch again.** Circle **T** for True or **F** for False.

1	It often rains in Antarctica.	**T**	**F**
2	The world's largest sheet of ice is in Antarctica.	**T**	**F**
3	Some whales live in Antarctica.	**T**	**F**
4	Explorers began studying Antarctica 20 years ago.	**T**	**F**

C   **Complete the summary below.** Use one word for each answer.

Antarctica is the coldest, windiest, and [1] _____ continent in the world. In [2] _____, temperatures can go below -40°C. Thousands of tourists visit Antarctica every year. It's beautiful and has many amazing seabirds, such as [3] _____. Many [4] _____ and explorers are studying the weather and the animals here.

After You Watch

Talk with a partner. What other extreme places on Earth do you know about? Describe them.

Penguins on an iceberg in Antarctica

A Complete the sentences. Use the correct form of the words in the box.

| flow | species | less | gentle | fast |

1 A river _____ next to my town.

2 Math is my _____ favorite subject.

3 Cats make good pets—they are _____ .

4 The cheetah is _____ land animal in the world.

5 The Amazon has some of the rarest _____ of plants.

B Complete the sentences. Use the correct form of the words in parentheses.

1 _____ (*large*) ice sheet in the world is in Antarctica.

2 I think that Paris is _____ (*exciting*) city in the world.

3 This garden has some of _____ (*pretty*) flowers in town.

4 What's _____ (*easy*) way to get to the museum?

5 _____ (*small*) town in my country has _____ (*good*) restaurant.

C Write the numbers in words.

1 3,000,000 _____

2 5,000,000,000 _____

3 ½ _____

4 2,300 _____

SELF CHECK Now I can …

☐ compare three or more things

☐ use language for describing extreme places and things

☐ talk about the Amazon

5

ARE PARROTS *SMARTER THAN PEOPLE?*

PREVIEW

A **Read the unit title.** Do you think parrots are smarter than people? Why or why not?

B 🎧 5.1 **Listen.** Circle **T** for True or **F** for False.

1 African gray parrots can count.　　　　　**T**　**F**

2 Horses can recognize human faces.　　　**T**　**F**

3 Border collies look after sheep on farms.　**T**　**F**

4 Dogs can remember things for longer　　**T**　**F**
　periods of time than cats.

A male African gray parrot

Talk with a partner. Which animal do you think is the smartest? Why?

> Horses are the smartest because they can solve problems.

> I think border collies are the smartest because they can learn rules quickly.

UNIT GOALS

- describe smart animals

- use language for comparing two things

- describe how animals use tools

55

LANGUAGE FOCUS

A 🎧 **5.2 Listen and read.** What pet does Stig have? Then repeat the conversation and replace the words in **bold**.

Ming: I really love dogs. Do you have a pet?

Stig: Yes, I do. It's really **cute**. Do you want to see it? (**playful / intelligent**)

Ming: Sure!

Stig: It has a funny dog face, but it's **smaller** than a dog. (**gentler / friendlier**)

Ming: It looks like a dog, but it's **smaller** than a dog? (**gentler / friendlier**)

Stig: Ta-da!

Ming: But … that's not a dog, that's a fish!

Stig: It's **better** than a fish, it's a dogface pufferfish! (**more interesting / more beautiful**)

B 🎧 **5.3 Look at the chart.** Circle the correct answers below.

MAKING COMPARISONS (USING COMPARATIVE ADJECTIVES)		
Horses are **faster than** dogs. I think cats are **more interesting than** fish.		tall → tall**er**
		bi**g** → bi**gg**er
Which are **more playful**, rabbits or turtles?	Rabbits are **more playful than** turtles, but turtles are **friendlier than** rabbits. **Both** rabbits **and** turtles are playful.	friend**ly** → friend**li**er
		intelligent → **more** intelligent
		good → **better**
		bad → **worse**

1 For short adjectives (e.g., *fast)*, we usually **add -*er* to the end** / **use *more* + adjective**.

2 For longer adjectives (e.g., *playful)*, we usually **add -*er* to the end** / **use *more* + adjective**.

3 We start a sentence with *I think* when we are **giving an opinion** / **stating a fact**.

C 🎧 5.4 **Complete the conversation.** Then listen and check your answers.

Grace: Hey Sam, I heard you have a new pet. What is it?

Sam: It's a rabbit.

Grace: My neighbor has a new pet lizard. He says it's [1] _____ (*interesting*) a pet cat.

Sam: That's cool. I heard some people have spiders and snakes for pets.

Grace: Wow! Which do you think are [2] _____ (*scary*), spiders or snakes?

Sam: Well, snakes are [3] _____ (*big*) spiders, but I think spiders are [4] _____ (*scary*) snakes.

D **Answer the questions.**

1 Which are bigger, elephants or mice? _____ Elephants are bigger than mice _____ .

2 Which are stronger, mice or rhinos? _____ .

3 Which are more intelligent, dolphins or chickens? _____ .

4 Which are friendlier, dogs or bears? _____ .

E **Work with a partner.** Play animal bingo. Choose nine animals from the box and write them in the chart below. Don't show your partner. Ask questions by picking any two animals from your chart and comparing them. Draw a circle around the animals that your partner says. Take turns. The first player with three circles in a straight line wins.

| fish | cat | shark | elephant | spider | lizard | dog | monkey | snake | bird |

ANIMAL BINGO

Example:

ANIMAL BINGO

(fish)	monkey	bird
(cat)	(elephant)	spider
shark	dog	(snake)

Which are more dangerous, sharks or snakes?

I think snakes are more dangerous.

THE REAL WORLD

SEA OTTERS AND THEIR KITCHEN TOOLS

A sea otter opens a clam.

A **Talk with a partner.** Look at the chart below. Which animals use tools the most? Which animals use tools the least? Can you think of other animals that use tools?

TABLE 1: ANIMALS AND HOW THEY USE TOOLS				
Ways of using tools	Chimpanzees	Birds	Insects	Fish
Throwing	✓	✓	✓	✓
Carrying objects to use	✓	✓	✓	✓
Hammering	✓	✓	✓	
Digging	✓	✓		
Cutting	✓			

B ▶ 5.1 **Watch the video.** Circle **T** for True or **F** for False.

1 Many marine animals use tools.   **T**   **F**

2 Sea otters use rocks as tools to open mussels.   **T**   **F**

3 To open mussels, sea otters throw rocks at them.   **T**   **F**

C ▶ 5.1 **Watch again.** Circle the correct words.

1 Sea otters can eat up to 75 mussels in one **hour** / **day**.

2 Sea otters eat the **soft bodies** / **hard shells** of mussels.

3 Sea otters sometimes place rocks on their **backs** / **bellies**.

D [CRITICAL THINKING Applying] **Look at the chart on page 58.** How do you think animals use tools?

PROJECT Make a list. Record five tools you use every day. How do they help you?

PRONUNCIATION reduction: *than*

🎧 5.5 **Listen.** Complete the sentences. Then take turns reading the sentences.

1 Cats are more independent _____.

2 Turtles are slower _____.

3 Are dogs cuter _____?

4 Fish are quieter _____.

5 Spiders are scarier _____.

COMMUNICATION

Work with a partner. Make a list of animals. Compare the animals using the adjectives in the box.

| interesting | beautiful | lazy | smart | friendly | scary |

LIST OF ANIMALS

I think cats are more interesting than parrots, but parrots are more beautiful than cats.

A rat uses its nose to find a land mine in Mozambique.

READING

A Skim the article. The article is about _____.
a rare animals
b how animals help people
c how people train animals

B Scan the article again. Underline things a therapy animal does.

C Talk with a partner. Do you know about other working animals? What do they do?

WORKING ANIMALS

🎧 **5.6** Some animals make great **pets**. They're friendly, fun, and smart. Other animals have special **jobs**—they're working animals.

Land Mine Rats

5 Rats can save lives. They have an incredible sense of smell. This helps them to find land mines. One rat can search over 200 square meters of ground in an hour. A person **spends** 50 hours to do the same job!

Therapy Animals

10 Therapy animals make people feel better. Cats, dogs, mice, rabbits, birds, and even hedgehogs can be therapy animals. Some hospitals use them to help **sick** people get **well**. Therapy animals hang out with lonely people and make them feel happier.
15 They go everywhere with their owners, sometimes even on airplanes!

Rescue Dogs

Rescue dogs help people **in trouble**. They can find people in the mountains, in the desert, and deep
20 under the snow. They can even find people under buildings after an earthquake. A common type of rescue dog is the German shepherd. These dogs are stronger and more intelligent than other dogs. They have stronger noses, too.

COMPREHENSION

A Answer the questions about _Working Animals_.

1   DETAIL   Rats are good at finding land mines because they have a good sense of _____ .

   a sight   **b** hearing   **c** smell

2   PURPOSE   Why does the author write about how long it takes for a rat and a person to do the same job?

   a to show that rats are smarter than humans

   b to show that rats are faster than humans

   c to show that rats and humans can do the same task

3   DETAIL   Therapy animals do all of the following EXCEPT _____ .

   a make people feel happier

   b help people to become well again

   c help their owners to get from one place to another

4   REFERENCE   In line 18, _people in trouble_ refers to people who _____ .

   a cannot swim   **b** cannot see   **c** need help

5   INFERENCE   A German shepherd is more likely to _____ .

   a look for lost people

   b help sick people get well

   c make lonely people feel happier

B Complete the summary below. Choose one word from the article for each answer.

Working animals have special ¹ _____ . Land mine ² _____ help us to find land mines. ³ _____ animals, such as hedgehogs, help sick people to get well. Some German shepherds are ⁴ _____ dogs—they can find people in trouble.

A woman holds a hedgehog.

C   CRITICAL THINKING Evaluating
Talk with a partner. Which group of working animals is the most useful to us? Why?

VOCABULARY

A Find the words below in the article. Then match the words with their meanings.

1 pet   ○   ○ healthy

2 job   ○   ○ having problems

3 spend   ○   ○ an animal you keep at home

4 sick   ○   ○ use time or money to do something

5 well   ○   ○ not healthy

6 in trouble   ○   ○ work you do to get money

IDIOM

If someone is "a wolf in sheep's clothing," they _____.
a seem friendly, but are dangerous
b seem more powerful than they actually are

B Read the information below. Then circle the two synonyms in each group.

> A synonym is a word that has a similar meaning to another word. For example, *small* and *little*.

1 fast   quick   slow

2 search   walk   look for

3 sad   ill   sick

4 save   improve   rescue

5 incredible amazing   common

DO YOU KNOW?

Penguins are _____ on land than in the sea.
a more active
b slower

WRITING

A Look at the blog post. Read the beginning of the post.

B Describe your favorite pet or other animal. What do you like about it?

C Write a blog post about your favorite animal. Give reasons why it's better or more interesting than other animals.

HOME   ABOUT US   BLOG   FAQ   CONTACT US

IGUANAS ARE THE BEST PETS!

Iguanas are great pets because they are special. Many people have dogs and cats, but not iguanas! Iguanas are cleaner than rabbits because . . .

HOW **CATS JUMP**

Before You Watch

Make a guess. A cat can jump up to _____ times its own height.

a two   **b** six   **c** ten

While You Watch

A ▶ **5.2** **Watch the video.** Match the names to the descriptions.

1 Missy   ○   ○ slipped and fell.

2 Steve   ○   ○ jumped onto a table.

3 Mr. Waffles ○   ○ jumped and hit a window.

B ▶ **5.2** **Watch again.** Number the steps in order (1–4). How does a cat jump onto a table?

_____ It prepares its body to make a jump.

_____ It uses its claws to stop.

_____ Its back legs push down and backwards on the ground.

_____ It pulls itself up onto the table.

C **Complete the summary below.** Use the words in the box.

hunt	light	back	house

Cats have amazing jumping skills. They are very [1] _____ , and use their powerful
[2] _____ legs to jump. In the wild, cats use their jumping skills to
[3] _____ . [4] _____ cats like to hunt, too.

After You Watch

Talk with a partner. How far can you jump? Which animals can jump farther or higher than you can?

A house cat jumps from
one chimney to another.

A **Complete the sentences.** Circle the correct answers.

Horses are my favorite animals. Some people keep them as
¹ **jobs** / **pets**. I think horses are more ² **playful** / **worse** than
most animals. They are very ³ **intelligent** / **scary**—they can
solve problems. Some hospitals use horses to help ⁴ **lost** / **sick**
people get well.

B **Complete the sentences.** Use the words given.

1 whales / heavy / turtles

   _____ .

2 interesting / parrots or cats

   _____ ?

3 both / rats and dogs / smart

   _____ .

4 dolphins / large / sea otters

   _____ .

C **Complete the sentences.** Use the correct form of the words
in the box.

ill	quick	rescue	incredible	search

1 It's _____ to drive there than to take the bus.

2 Sofia is not in school today—she's _____ .

3 Kei is _____ for his wallet in the classroom.

4 Norman is a(n) _____ dog—he can ride a bicycle!

5 I _____ a cat from a tree last night.

SELF CHECK   Now I can ...

☐ describe smart animals

☐ use language for comparing two things

☐ describe how animals use tools

I REALLY LIKE ELECTRONIC MUSIC!

PREVIEW

A 🎧 6.1 **Listen.** Number the type of music you hear in order.

__1__	jazz	○	○ Louis
____	rap	○	○ Jo
____	pop	○	○ Marcus
____	classical	○	○ Paco
____	rock	○	○ May
____	electronic	○	○ Anna

B 🎧 6.2 **Listen.** Match each type of music to the person who likes it.

C **Talk with a partner.** Ask about their favorite type of music.

What kind of music do you like?

I like rock.

HISTORY AND CULTURE

German electronic music duo Modeselektor performs in Copenhagen, Denmark.

UNIT GOALS

• describe different types of music

• use language for expressing your opinions

• describe how music affects your brain

LANGUAGE FOCUS

A 🎧 **6.3** **Listen and read.** What kind of music are Stig and Ming listening to? Then repeat the conversation and replace the words in **bold**.

REAL ENGLISH Not exactly.

Ming: Hey, what are you listening to?

Stig: I'm listening to some **awesome** new music! (**cool / great**)

Ming: Cool! What kind of music is it?

Stig: It's **pop**. (**rock / jazz**)

Ming: I really like **pop**. Did you just buy it? (**rock / jazz**)

Stig: Uh … not exactly. It just came out last week. Here, listen.

Ming: This is terrible. I **don't like it at all**. Who is this? (**really don't like it / can't stand it**)

Stig: Actually, it's my band!

B 🎧 **6.4** **Look at the chart.** Circle the correct answers below.

GIVING AND EXPRESSING OPINIONS (USING *LIKE*)	
Do you like Imagine Dragons? Do you like Bruno Mars / Katy Perry? Do you like rap?	Yes, I love **them**! Yes, I like **him** / **her**. No, I can't stand **it**.
What kind of music **do** you **like (the) best**?	I really **like** jazz. / I **like** rock **(the) best**.
Which do you **like better**, pop **or** rock? **Who** do you **like better**, Ed Sheeran **or** Billie Eilish?	I **like** rock **better**. I like Ed Sheeran **better**.

1 When we talk about a singer, you say, "I like **he (or she)** / **him (or her)**."

2 If you really don't like a type of music, you can't stand **it** / **them**.

3 If you listen to one kind of music all the time, you like it **better** / **the best**.

C 🎧 **6.5** **Listen.** Complete the chart by coloring in the stars.

	ROCK	RAP	CLASSICAL	POP
Ana	☆ ☆ ☆ ☆	☆ ☆ ☆ ☆	☆ ☆ ☆ ☆	☆ ☆ ☆ ☆
Yoko	☆ ☆ ☆ ☆	☆ ☆ ☆ ☆	☆ ☆ ☆ ☆	☆ ☆ ☆ ☆
Carl	☆ ☆ ☆ ☆	☆ ☆ ☆ ☆	☆ ☆ ☆ ☆	☆ ☆ ☆ ☆

★★★★	I love it.
★★★☆	I like it.
★★☆☆	It's OK.
★☆☆☆	I don't like it.
☆☆☆☆	I can't stand it.

D 🎧 **6.5** **Listen again.** Answer the questions. Use the information in **C**.

1 Does Ana like classical music? ___No, she can't stand it___ .

2 Does Ana like pop? _____ .

3 Does Yoko like rock? _____ .

4 Which does Yoko like better, classical music or pop? _____ .

5 Does Carl like rap? _____ .

6 What music does Carl like best? _____ .

E **Work with a partner.** Complete the conversation with your own ideas. Then take turns reading the conversation. Repeat with different types of music and singers.

A: Sorry, but can you change the music? I can't stand it.

B: Sure. I have other kinds of music. Which do you like better, _____ (**type of music**) or _____ (**type of music**)?

A: I like _____ (**type of music**) better.

B: Then how about _____ (**singer or band**)? Do you like _____ (**him / her / them**)?

A: Oh, I love _____ (**him / her / them**)!

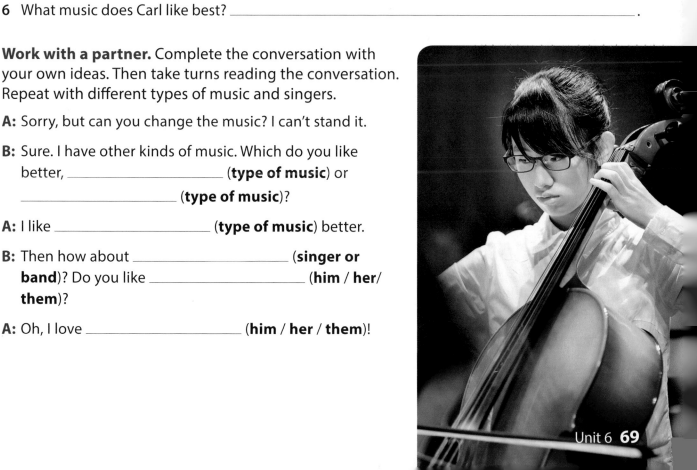

YOUR **BRAIN** ON **MUSIC**

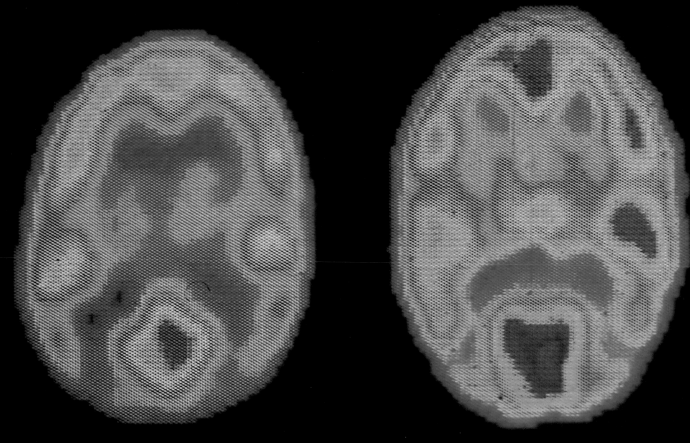

RESTING   LISTENING TO MUSIC

The red and yellow areas of these scans show brain activity.

A **Look at the brain scans.** Which task causes our brain to be more active?

    a resting   **b** listening to music

B ▶ 6.1 **Watch Part 1 of the video.** Brain scientist David Poeppel shows how music can make us think of certain colors. Write the color you thought of for each piece of music you hear. Then compare your results with the class.

Piece 1	Piece 2	Piece 3

DO YOU KNOW?

Our brain responds to music the same way it responds to

_____.

a food
b stress

C ▶6.2 **Watch Part 2 of the video.** Did you choose the same colors as most people? Complete the sentences.

   1 More than 70% of people thought of the color _____ when they heard the first piece.

   2 For the second piece, the majority of people picked the color _____ .

   3 For the third piece, the majority of people chose the color _____ .

D CRITICAL THINKING Personalizing **Talk with a partner.** What's your favorite type of music? What color does it make you think of?

> **PROJECT Do an experiment.** As a group, create a list of ten different pieces of music. Then listen. For each piece, write the color you think of. Count the results. How many students chose the same colors?

PRONUNCIATION syllable stress

A 🎧6.6 **Listen.** Write the number of syllables.

   1 <u>terrible</u> ___3___   **2** awesome _____   **3** important _____

   4 intelligent _____   **5** different _____   **6** dangerous _____

B 🎧6.6 **Listen again and underline the stressed syllable.** Then read the words to a partner.

COMMUNICATION

Work in a group. Do a survey. Ask your group members to rate each kind of music using the chart below. Find out the most popular kind of music in your group.

Kinds of Music	You	_____	_____	_____	Total Points
Rap					
Jazz					
Rock					
Electronic					
Classical					

0: I can't stand it.	**1:** I don't really like it.	**2:** It's all right/OK.	**3:** I like it.	**4:** I love it.

Do you like jazz?   No, I don't really like it.

Evelyn performs at the opening ceremony of the London 2012 Olympic Games.

READING

A **Skim the article.** Why is Evelyn Glennie a special musician?

B **Scan the article.** What musical instruments did Evelyn learn to play? Circle them.

C **Talk with a partner.** What other musical instruments do you know about? Can you play any?

THE FEEL OF
MUSIC

A 🎧 **6.7** One of the world's most famous musicians "hears" through her feet. Evelyn Glennie is deaf—she cannot hear. But she can sense music. She feels movement of sounds through the **floor**.

B As a child, Evelyn learned to play different musical **instruments**, such as the harmonica. She was also a good piano student. But when she was eight, she started to have hearing problems. That did not stop Evelyn's love for music. She found another way to play music. She realized that she could "hear" notes in her feet and body.

C At age 12, Evelyn **decided** to take up drum lessons after she saw a friend play. At 16, she studied at a **well-known** music college in England. She graduated in three years. At 23, she won her first Grammy Award. She is the first person in musical history to have a career as a solo percussionist.

D Evelyn now **performs** at **concerts** all over the world. She works with orchestras in the United States and Europe, and also teaches other musicians. She performs and practices with no shoes on. And, as a collector of percussion instruments, she owns more than 2,000 drums and other instruments!

COMPREHENSION

IDIOM

If something is "music to your ears," you _____.
a are happy to hear it
b cannot understand it

A Answer the questions about *The Feel of Music*.

1 REFERENCE The word *That* in the fourth sentence of paragraph B refers to _____.

   a Evelyn turning eight

   b Evelyn's hearing problems

   c Evelyn's ability to play the piano

2 DETAIL Evelyn _____ music when she lost her hearing.

   a stopped playing   b didn't give up   c decided to learn

3 INFERENCE Evelyn doesn't wear shoes when she performs so that she _____.

   a can move quickly   b feels relaxed   c can feel the music

4 MAIN IDEA Paragraph D is mainly about _____.

   a what Evelyn does now

   b what Evelyn did as a child

   c what musical instruments Evelyn can play

5 DETAIL Which of the following is NOT in the article?

   a Evelyn's age when she won her first Grammy Award

   b the number of concerts Evelyn plays in a year

   c the length of time Evelyn spent in music college

B Match. Which paragraph contains the following information?

1 The type of musical instruments Evelyn collects ○   ○ Paragraph B

2 When Evelyn started to have hearing problems ○   ○ Paragraph C

3 Where Evelyn studied music   ○   ○ Paragraph D

C CRITICAL THINKING Inferring **Read the quote by Evelyn Glennie below.** What do you think she means?

"My hearing is out of the ordinary as others might see it, but not for me. I'm used to my hearing in the same way that I'm used to the size of my hands."

VOCABULARY

A Find the words below in the article. Then complete the sentences using the correct form of the words in the box.

floor	instrument	decide	well-known	perform	concert

Evelyn is a(n) ¹ _____ musician. When she was young, she learned to play different musical ² _____ . She lost her hearing at a young age, but she
³ _____ to take up drum lessons. She cannot hear, but she can feel sounds moving through the ⁴ _____ . In 2012, she ⁵ _____ in the opening ceremony of the Olympic Games. In 2015, she played a(n) ⁶ _____ for her 50th birthday.

B Read the information below. Then complete the sentences with the correct collective nouns.

> We use collective nouns to describe different groups of people;
> for example, *audience*, *band*, *class*, *crowd*, and *team*.

1 The _____ enjoyed Evelyn's concert.

2 The teacher gave homework to her _____ .

3 Ana and her friends recently started a jazz _____ .

4 A large _____ gathered outside the restaurant.

5 The school's ice hockey _____ won the match yesterday.

WRITING

A Look at the music review. Read the beginning of the review.

B Listen to a new song or album or watch a music performance. Make notes about it.

C Write a music review. Describe the song or album or performance. Use your notes from **B**.

JS **Julia Santos**
@juliasantos   ⌄

I love the new album by Billie Eilish. I like to listen to it at night before I go to bed. Billie Eilish is more interesting than many other singers. I really like her strong voice, and the music is relaxing …

👍 Like   💬 Comment   ➤ Share

ME | Write a comment...   📷 ☺

THE **MUSICAL** MAGIC OF **ICE**

Before You Watch

Talk to a partner. Think of a few musical instruments. What materials are they made of?

While You Watch

A ▶ 6.3 **Watch the video.** According to the video, what are the two disadvantages of ice musical instruments? Check (✓) your answers.

☐ They melt easily.

☐ They are too cold for musicians to hold.

☐ They take a long time to make.

☐ They sound different after a while.

B ▶ 6.3 **Watch again.** Circle the correct answers.

1 Tim's dream was to have an ice **hotel** / **music concert**.

2 **Heat** / **Snow** causes Tim's ice musical instruments to sound different.

3 Tim built a **concert hall** / **music school**.

C Discuss with a partner. Read the statements below. Which of these people do you think are most likely to go to an ice music concert? Why?

• Leah is a student and she loves classical music.

• Jake is an explorer. He often takes photos of interesting places.

• Min is an engineer. She goes to the movies every weekend.

• Juan is a violin prodigy. He loves to travel and explore new places.

After You Watch

Talk with a partner. Do you know of any musical instruments made from unusual materials?

A musician plays the ice horn in Hokkaido, Japan.

A Complete the words.

1 A type of music

____ ____ *a* ____ ____ *i* *c* ____ ____

2 An object you use to play music

____ *n* ____ ____ ____ *m* ____ *n* ____

3 Famous

w ____ ____ *l* - ____ ____ *o* ____ ____

4 To act, dance, or sing for a group of people

____ ____ *r* ____ ____ *r* ____

B Write the sentences. Use the words given.

1 like / pop / best / the

I _____ .

2 stand / rock / can't / music

I _____ .

3 like / jazz / do / better / you /pop / or

Which _____ ?

4 kind / best / the / music / of / do / like / you

What _____ ?

C Complete the sentences. Circle the correct answers.

1 In a class, people **learn** / **eat** together.

2 People in a band play **music** / **a sport** together.

3 A crowd is a **small** / **big** group of people in a public place.

4 People in an audience **sing in** / **watch** a performance together.

5 People in a team play a sport **together** / **against one another**.

SELF CHECK Now I can …

☐ describe different types of music

☐ use language for expressing my opinions

☐ describe how music affects my brain

7

WHAT'S FOR DINNER?

PREVIEW

A 🎧 7.1 **Listen.** Check (✓) the foods and drinks you hear.

- ☐ honey
- ☐ tuna
- ☐ bread
- ☐ crabs
- ☐ milk
- ☐ tomatoes
- ☐ berries
- ☐ oranges
- ☐ meat

B 🎧 7.1 **Listen again.** Where do the people in each place get their food? Match.

1 Malaysia ○   ○ from farms and forests

2 Greece ○   ○ from hunting and fishing

3 East Africa ○   ○ from hunting and gathering

People around the world eat different kinds of food.

Talk with a partner. What did you eat yesterday?

> What did you have for dinner last night?

> I had fish and a salad. How about you?

UNIT GOALS

- describe different foods
- use language for talking about countable and uncountable things
- learn how taste works

79

LANGUAGE FOCUS

A **🎧7.2** **Listen and read.** What did Stig and Nadine get for the class party? Then repeat the conversation and replace the words in **bold**.

> REAL ENGLISH I can't wait!

Stig: I can't wait for the class party! Oh, let's get some **cookies**. (**cupcakes / ice cream**)

Nadine: I made a list. First, we need bread, cheese, and meat.

Stig: Uh-huh, meat, sure.

Nadine: OK. We need some **plates**. And something to eat with, like forks. (**napkins / cups**)

Stig: Yeah, sure.

Nadine: I think we need some **juice**. Last year we didn't have any. (**soda / bottled water**)

Stig: **Juice**. OK, here's some. (**Soda / Bottled water**)

Stig: Great! I think we have everything.

Nadine: Wait a minute. These are all snacks! We didn't get any **real food**! (**cheese / bread**)

B **🎧7.3** **Look at the chart.** Circle the correct answers below.

EXPRESSING EXISTENCE (USING *THERE IS, THERE ARE*)			
Countable nouns		**Uncountable nouns**	
There are some plates on the table. **There aren't any** forks.		**There's some** juice on the counter. **There isn't any** ice cream in the refrigerator.	
Are there any apples?	Yes, **there are**. No, **there aren't**.	**Is there any** salad?	Yes, **there is**. No, **there isn't**.

1   Rice, milk, and soda are examples of **countable / uncountable** nouns.

2   Eggs, potatoes, and strawberries are examples of **countable / uncountable** nouns.

3   We usually use the **plural / singular** form to talk about an uncountable noun.

C **Look at the picture.** Complete the sentences.

1 _There aren't any_ napkins on the table.

2 _____ plates in the sink.

3 _____ soda on the counter.

4 _____ glasses in the sink.

5 _____ knives on the table.

6 _____ milk in the refrigerator.

D **Work with a partner.** Look at the picture above. Complete the questions on your own. Then take turns asking and answering.

1 _____ milk on the counter?

2 _____ bowls in the sink?

3 _____?

4 _____?

5 _____?

E **Work in a group.** Play a game. **Student A:** Make a list of ten things in your refrigerator. **Students B**, **C**, and **D:** Take turns guessing what is in Student A's refrigerator. If you make three incorrect guesses, you are out of the game.

> Is there any orange juice in your refrigerator?

> No, there isn't.

> Are there any vegetables in your refrigerator?

THE **ART** (AND STYLE!) OF **FOOD**

A photographer takes photos and videos of food.

A ▶ 7.1 **Watch the video.** Check (✓) the foods you see.

☐ strawberry ☐ burger ☐ coffee ☐ ice cream ☐ tomato ☐ shrimp

B ▶ 7.1 **Watch again.** Check (✓) two correct answers. According to the video, what are some ways to make food look good in videos?

☐ film videos in slow motion ☐ paint the food

☐ use beautiful plates or glasses ☐ use good lighting

C **Complete the paragraph below.** Use the words in the box.

drinks	milk	ice cream	strawberries

Some of the things food stylists use to make food look good aren't actually food! They sometimes use white glue instead of [1] _____ so that breakfast cereal doesn't become soft. Or they add soap bubbles to [2] _____ to make them look more bubbly. Sometimes they paint [3] _____ with lipstick to make them look red. Finally, because [4] _____ melts quickly, food stylists often use frosting instead!

D CRITICAL THINKING Applying **Find any photo or video of food.** What do you think the food stylists did to make it more attractive?

> **PROJECT Photograph your food.** Work with a partner. For the next 24 hours, take photos of your meals. Then, show them to your partner and describe what you ate.

PRONUNCIATION linked sounds

🎧 7.4 **Listen.** Complete the sentences. Take turns reading the sentences.

1 There are some _____ the sink.

2 Are there any _____ the table?

3 There are some _____ the counter.

4 There are some _____ the cabinet.

COMMUNICATION

Work with a partner. Find the differences. **Student A:** Look at the picture below.
Student B: Look at the picture on page 151. Take turns asking and answering questions to find seven differences. Circle them.

Are there any noodles?

No, there aren't.

man makes pizza at a
zzeria in Seattle, USA.

READING

A **Look at the photo and read the headings.** What's the article about?

    a   the ingredients in pizza

    b   how people started making pizza

    c   how to make pizza

B **Scan the article.** Where was the first pizzeria?

C **Talk with a partner.** Do you like pizza? Why do you think it's popular?

A *SLICE* OF HISTORY

A 🎧 **7.5** What's your favorite pizza? Pepperoni? Meat? Veggie? Many people around the world love pizza. But where did it **come from**?

B **The First Pizza.** Every pizza has a crust. A crust is a **thin**, flat bread. Five to ten thousand years ago, people made flat bread on hot rocks. Then, someone decided to put other food, or toppings, on top of the flat bread. This was the world's first pizza.

C **Food for Soldiers.** About 2,500 years ago, the Persian army was a long way from home. The **hungry** soldiers did not have any ovens, so they cooked flat bread on their metal shields. They put **various** toppings on the bread.

D **Dangerous Tomatoes?** Explorers from South America brought tomatoes to Europe in the 1520s. At first, the Europeans thought tomatoes were poisonous. But people soon found out that tomatoes were safe … and **delicious**! Today, tomato sauce is a basic topping on pizza.

E **The First Pizzeria.** Pizza makers opened the world's first pizza restaurant, or pizzeria, in 1830, in Naples, Italy. The **chefs** used hot lava from a volcano to cook the pizza!

F **Pizza for the World.** In the late 19th century, many Italians moved to the United States. Some of them opened pizzerias, and pizza became very popular. Now, pizza is sold all over the world. People eat about 5 billion pizzas every year!

COMPREHENSION

A **Answer the questions about** *A Slice of History*.

1 **DETAIL** The Persian soldiers cooked flat bread _____ .

    a in ovens   **b** on their shields   **c** on the ground

2 **PURPOSE** Why does the author include the paragraph about tomatoes?

    a to show the history of tomatoes

    b to show that people from all over the world love pizza

    c to show where a key ingredient of pizza came from

> **IDIOM**
>
> "Your eyes are bigger than your stomach" means _____ .
> **a** you like looking at food
> **b** you can eat a lot
> **c** you take more food than you can eat

3 **INFERENCE** How are pizzas today similar to pizzas from 2,500 years ago?

    a they have a crust

    b people cook them in ovens

    c they use tomato sauce

4 **DETAIL** The first pizzeria was opened about _____ years ago.

    a 2,500   **b** 1,830   **c** 200

5 **MAIN IDEA** Paragraph F is mainly about how pizza _____ around the world.

    a is made   **b** became popular   **c** is different

B **Complete the timeline.** Write notes about the history of pizza.

History of Pizza

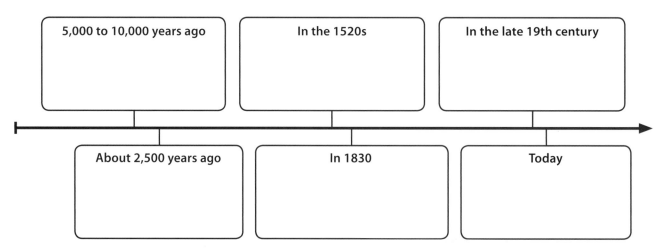

5,000 to 10,000 years ago	In the 1520s	In the late 19th century

About 2,500 years ago	In 1830	Today

C **CRITICAL THINKING Personalizing** **Talk with a partner.** Think of a popular dish you like. What are its ingredients?

VOCABULARY

A **Find the words below in the article.** Then complete the sentences using the correct form of the words in the box.

> come from   thin   hungry   various   delicious   chef

Pizza ¹ _____ Italy. It has a thick or ² _____ crust and toppings like cheese, meat, or vegetables. ³ _____ make ⁴ _____ kinds of pizza, such as plain, pepperoni, and Hawaiian. They are all ⁵ _____ ! Some ⁶ _____ people can finish a whole pizza by themselves.

B **Read the information below.** Then match the adjectives with the pictures.

> We use adjectives to describe how food tastes. For example, *bitter*, *salty*, *sour*, and *sweet*.

1 bitter ◯ ◯

2 salty ◯ ◯

3 sour ◯ ◯

4 sweet ◯ ◯

Hey, Vera! Where are you now? I'm getting ready for our family barbecue, but there isn't enough food. We have some fruit, bread, and meat. But we don't have any salad or juice. Please buy some on your way here.

Delivered

WRITING

A **Imagine you are preparing a barbecue.** Make a list of things that you need for the barbecue.

B **Read the text message.**

C **Write a text message.** Ask your friend or family member for help in buying the things you need.

HOW DO WE *TASTE* FOOD?

Before You Watch

Talk with a partner. Match the senses with the parts of the body. Then check (✓) the senses you think affect how food tastes.

| skin | eyes | tongue | nose | ears |

☐ sight _____   ☐ taste _____   ☐ sound _____

☐ smell _____   ☐ touch _____

While You Watch

A ▶ 7.2 **Watch the video.** Circle **T** for True or **F** for False.

1 More than 50% of what we think is taste is actually smell.   **T   F**

2 The study of how our brains taste food is called neuropsychology.   **T   F**

3 Food tastes sweeter when it's on a round plate.   **T   F**

B ▶ 7.2 **Watch again.** Match the colors of foods with how our brain thinks they taste.

1 red   ○   ○ salty

2 green ○   ○ sweet

3 black ○   ○ bitter

4 white ○   ○ sour

C **Complete the chart.** Circle the correct answers.

	Food	What we see	What we taste
1	lime	**black / green**	**bitter / sour**
2	strawberry	**red / white**	**sweet / salty**
3	popcorn	**green / white**	**salty / sour**
4	coffee	**black / green**	**sweet / bitter**

After You Watch

Talk with a partner. What are your favorite foods?
Are they of the same color?

These kinds of cauliflower are naturally colorful.

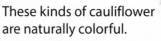

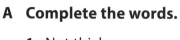

REVIEW

A Complete the words.

1 Not thick   t _ _ _ n

2 A sweet food that bees make   _ o _ _ e y

3 Many different   v _ r _ _ u s

4 A cold dish with many vegetables   s _ l _ d

5 A person who cooks food as a job   c _ _ f

B Complete the conversations. Circle the correct answers.

1 **Emma:** Let's bake a cake for the party tomorrow. [1] **Are / Is** there any eggs on the table?

  Zoe: No, there [2] **aren't / isn't**. Should I buy [3] **some / any**?

  Emma: Yes, please. Please buy some milk too—there [4] **aren't / isn't** any in the refrigerator.

2 **Marco:** I'm really hungry. [5] **Are / Is** there any sandwiches in the kitchen?

  Anna: Yes, there [6] **are / is**.

  Marco: Is there [7] **some / any** orange juice?

  Anna: No, there isn't. But there [8] **is / are** soda on the table.

C Complete the chart below. How do these foods taste? Use *bitter*, *salty*, *sour*, and *sweet*.

1 _____	2 _____	3 _____	4 _____
lime green apples	green tea coffee	honey cookies	fries cheese

---

SELF CHECK   Now I can …

☐ describe different foods

☐ use language for talking about countable and uncountable things

☐ explain how taste works

YOU *SHOULD* SEE A **DOCTOR!**

PREVIEW

A 🎧 8.1 **Listen.** Circle the body parts that Rick injured.

foot   hand   knee

arm   back   leg

B 🎧 8.2 **Listen.** Circle the correct answers.

1 Anton has a **backache** / **headache**.

2 Janet's sister **broke** / **cut** her leg.

3 Sonia has a **sore** / **broken** back.

4 Eric **hurt** / **broke** his knee when he fell. He **broke** / **cut** his hand, too.

C **Talk with a partner.** Talk about a time you hurt yourself.

> I cut my hand yesterday when I was cooking.

> Last month, I fell on the street. I hurt my knee.

A mountain biker falls off a bicycle.

SCIENCE AND TECHNOLOGY

UNIT GOALS

• ask for and give advice

• use language for talking about illnesses

• talk about how viruses spread

LANGUAGE FOCUS

A 🎧 **8.3** **Listen and read.** What's Stig's advice for treating sore throats? Then repeat the conversation and replace the words in **bold**.

REAL ENGLISH Come on!

Stig: Hey Ming, let's study for our science test. Hey, **what's wrong**? (**are you OK** / **are you all right**)

Ming: **I feel sick**. I have a headache. (**I'm sick** / **I don't feel well**)

Stig: You should take some medicine. Come on, the test is on Friday!

Ming: Uh, I also have a **sore throat**. (**cough** / **stomachache**)

Stig: Well, why don't you drink some tea? Let's go! We need to study.

Ming: Ow! My knee hurts, too!

Stig: OK, you should see a doctor. I'm calling one now.

Ming: The doctor? Uh … I feel **much better** now! (**OK** / **great**)

B 🎧 **8.4** **Look at the chart.** Circle the correct answers below.

ASKING FOR AND GIVING ADVICE (USING MODALS)	
Maya is sick. She has a sore throat. What **should** she **do**?	She **should** stay home and rest.
I have a cough. What **should** I **do**?	You **should** take some cough medicine.
	Why don't you take some cough medicine?
Emma and Kevin both have colds. **Should** they go to a doctor?	Yes, they **should**. No, they **shouldn't**.

1 To make a suggestion, we use "Why **do** / **don't** you?"

2 To give advice, we use *you should* + **base form** / **past tense**.

3 *Why don't you* means almost the same thing as *you **should*** / ***shouldn't***.

C Circle the correct answers.

1 Janice has a stomachache. She **should / shouldn't** see a doctor.

2 I hurt my foot. The doctor says I **should / shouldn't** rest for a week.

3 You look tired. **Should / Why don't** you get some rest?

4 Everyone is sleeping, so we **should / shouldn't** make a lot of noise.

5 Diego is good at drawing. **Should / Why don't** you ask him for help?

D 🎧 8.5 Complete the conversations. Use *should*, *shouldn't*, or *Why don't you*. Then listen and check your answers.

1 **Lucas:**   I have a headache. What ¹ _____ I do?

   Camila: ² _____ take some medicine?

2 **Maria:** I have a backache. What ³ _____ ?

   Peter: ⁴ _____ stay home and rest?

3 **Lee:**   Victor has a toothache. ⁵ _____ eat some ice cream?

   Erika: No, he ⁶ _____ .

4 **Ian:**   Lisa has an earache. ⁷ _____ stay home and rest?

   Kei: Yes, she ⁸ _____ . She ⁹ _____ go to work.

E Work in a group. Take turns acting out a health problem. Work together to guess the problem and give two suggestions.

Do you have a cough?

Yes, I do! What should I do?

BEATING **THE FLU**

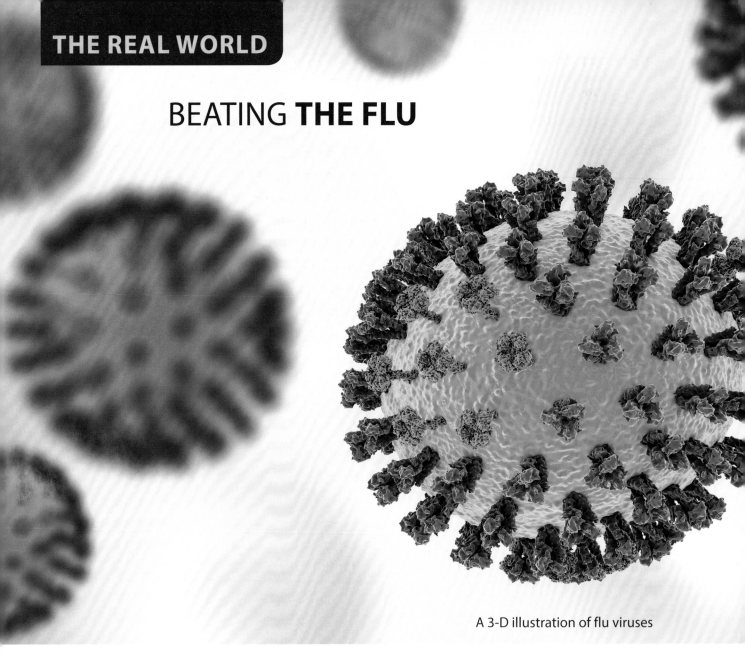

A 3-D illustration of flu viruses

A ▶ 8.1 **Watch the video.** Circle **T** for True or **F** for False.

1 Most of the time, flu spreads through the air.   **T**   **F**

2 A pandemic is an illness that affects a few people   **T**   **F**
over a large area.

3 There are more than 5,000 kinds of flu virus.   **T**   **F**

B ▶ 8.1 **Watch again.** Complete the sentences. Write a word for each answer.

1 Influenza is another name for the _____ virus.

2 The avian flu virus can spread from _____ to humans.

3 Between 1918 and 1919, the Spanish flu caused one _____ of the
people in the world to become ill.

C Complete the poster. Use the phrases in the box. Add two ideas of your own.

~~wash your hands often~~	get a flu vaccination	go outside when you're sick
~~rub your eyes~~	touch your face	cover your mouth when you cough

HELP **PREVENT** THE **FLU**

DOs	DON'Ts
✓ Wash your hands often.	✗ Don't rub your eyes.
✓	✗
✓	✗
✓	✗

D [CRITICAL THINKING Analyzing] **Talk with a partner.** Viruses now spread more quickly and reach wider areas than 200 years ago. Why do you think this is?

PROJECT Do a survey. Ask your friends how many times a year they usually get sick. Make a chart.

PRONUNCIATION *should, could, would*

A 🎧 8.6 **Listen and repeat.**

1 should, shouldn't   2 could, couldn't   3 would, wouldn't

B 🎧 8.7 **Listen.** Write the words you hear. Take turns reading the sentences.

1 If Danny has a cold, he _____ rest.   3 They _____ play soccer in the rain.

2 I _____ hear what she was saying.   4 _____ you like some orange juice?

COMMUNICATION

Work in a group of four. Do a survey on healthy habits. Turn to page 152 and follow the instructions.

Do you get plenty of sleep?

Yes, I do.

Ingredients in traditional Chinese medicine

READING

A **Skim the article.** What's the article about?
a   the chemicals in medicine
b   how people grow herbs
c   why scientists today study traditional medicine

B **Scan the article.** What did ancient Egyptians use to treat pain?

C **Talk with a partner.** Does your family use any traditional remedies? What are they?

Old New Medicines

A 🎧 **8.8** What should you do if you have a headache? In **modern** times, people often take aspirin. But is aspirin actually a modern medicine?

B More than 4,000 years ago, ancient Egyptians used dried leaves to treat **pain**. And in the fourth **century** B.C., people used a medicine made from tree bark to treat fevers. In the nineteenth century, European scientists discovered that both remedies **contain** the same chemical. They used the chemical to make a modern drug—aspirin. Today, it's one of the world's cheapest and most helpful drugs.

C Some of the drugs we have today come from traditional Chinese medicine. In the third century B.C., healers began studying the human body. They tested various treatments and recorded their effects on **patients**. For more than 2,000 years, doctors recorded what they learned in books. These ancient books are still useful today. Tu Youyou, a Chinese medical researcher, found that in the past, people used wormwood—a herb with yellow flowers—to treat fevers. After studying it, she **developed** a drug—artemisinin—that saved millions of people from dying of malaria.

D For centuries, Western medicine paid little attention to traditional Chinese medicine. But today, scientists are studying traditional treatments to develop modern cures for diseases such as cancer.

COMPREHENSION

A **Answer the questions about *Old New Medicines*.**

1 **MAIN IDEA** Paragraph B is mainly about _____ .

   a how traditional remedies work

   b why people use modern medicine

   c the history of the chemical we use to make aspirin

2 **DETAIL** Aspirin can treat all of the following EXCEPT _____ .

   a headaches   **b** malaria   **c** fevers

3 **REFERENCE** The word *it* in the last sentence of paragraph C refers to _____ .

   a wormwood   **b** fever   **c** an ancient book

4 **INFERENCE** Which of the following was true about Western medicine in the past?

   a It was cheaper than traditional Chinese medicine.

   b It often used traditional Chinese herbs.

   c It was not based on the science behind traditional Chinese medicine.

5 **DETAIL** Which of the following is NOT in the article?

   a herbs doctors can use to treat cancer

   b the things early doctors recorded in books

   c the name of the person who developed artemisinin

B **Match the medicines with the descriptions.**

1 Aspirin is   ○   ○ a drug for malaria.

2 Wormwood is   ○   ○ a modern medicine for headaches.

3 Artemisinin is   ○   ○ a herb.

C **CRITICAL THINKING Personalizing** **Talk with a partner.** Do you prefer traditional remedies or modern medicine? Why?

Wormwood

VOCABULARY

IDIOM

"I'm worried sick" means

_____.

a I'm very worried
b I need to see a doctor

A **Find the words below in the article.** Then complete the sentences using the correct form of the words in the box.

| modern | pain | century |
| contain | patient | develop |

1 Some doctors use herbs to treat _____ with cancer.

2 A _____ is a period of 100 years.

3 Scientists are _____ vaccines against flu viruses.

4 Ian went to the doctor—he has back _____.

5 Fruits and vegetables _____ a lot of water.

6 Email is a _____ way to communicate with friends.

B **Read the information below.** Then complete the sentences with the correct form of *catch*, *look after*, *recover*, or *take*.

> We use some verbs to talk about health.
>
> *catch:* get a disease
>
> *look after:* take care of
>
> *recover:* become well again
>
> *take* something: swallow or drink medicine

1 Jun is not feeling well, he should _____ some medicine.

2 Mari _____ a cold last night.

3 Sofia has to _____ her three sons.

4 Carl is _____ from a broken arm.

WRITING

A **Look at the magazine article.** Read the beginning of the article.

B **Choose a health problem to write about.** Make notes. Go online to find information about it.

C **Write a short article for a teen magazine.** Give some advice on the health problem. Use your notes from **B**.

HOME   ABOUT US   **ARTICLES**   FAQ   CONTACT U

WAYS TO REDUCE STRESS

1 Get more sleep

You should get seven to nine hours of sleep every night.

2 Exercise

Exercise reduces stress. You should exercise …

BIKING *IN* CITIES

Before You Watch

Talk with a partner. Do you think people should bike in cities? What are the advantages and disadvantages?

While You Watch

A   ▶8.2   **Watch the video.** Choose the sentence that best describes the video.

   a   Air pollution comes from vehicles.

   b   Exercise is good for us.

   c   Biking in places with air pollution is sometimes unhealthy.

B   ▶8.2   **Watch again.** Read the sentences. Circle **T** for True and **F** for False.

   1   We breathe in more pollution when we exercise.   **T**   **F**

   2   The special shirt in the study measures the cyclist's speed.   **T**   **F**

   3   The scientists want to create an app that shows bike routes with less pollution.   **T**   **F**

C   **Circle the correct answer.** Which of the following do you think the scientists would be most interested in?

   a   safety equipment for bikers

   b   health effects of air pollution on children in cities

   c   ways to reduce air pollution from factories

After You Watch

Talk with a partner. What are some other ways that exercise can be bad for our bodies?

A group of cyclists in Paris, France

REVIEW

A **Complete the sentences.** Circle the correct answers.

1 Anna has a cold—she should _____ at home.
   a hurt   **b** cut   **c** rest

2 Scientists use _____ technology to measure air pollution.
   a modern   **b** century   **c** early

3 A group of scientists is _____ a smartphone app that measures air pollution.
   a containing   **b** developing   **c** breaking

4 She ate too much food, so she has a _____ now.
   a stomachache   **b** backache   **c** cough

B **Complete the conversation.** Circle the correct words.

Jin: Ling has a fever. What should she ¹ **does / do**?

Yanni: She ² **should / shouldn't** take some medicine.

Ana: Why don't we ³ **visit / to visit** her?

Jin: No, we ⁴ **should / shouldn't** do that. She needs to rest.

C **Complete the conversation.** Use the correct form of *catch*, *look*, *recover*, or *take*.

Matias: Hey Juan, are you coming to school today?

Juan: No, I ¹ _____ a cold over the weekend. I'm still ² _____ from it.

Matias: Did you ³ _____ any medicine?

Juan: Yes, I did.

Matias: Are you alone?

Juan: No, my mother's here to ⁴ _____ after me.

SELF CHECK   Now I can …

☐ ask for and give advice

☐ use language for talking about illnesses

☐ talk about how viruses spread

Unit 8   **101**

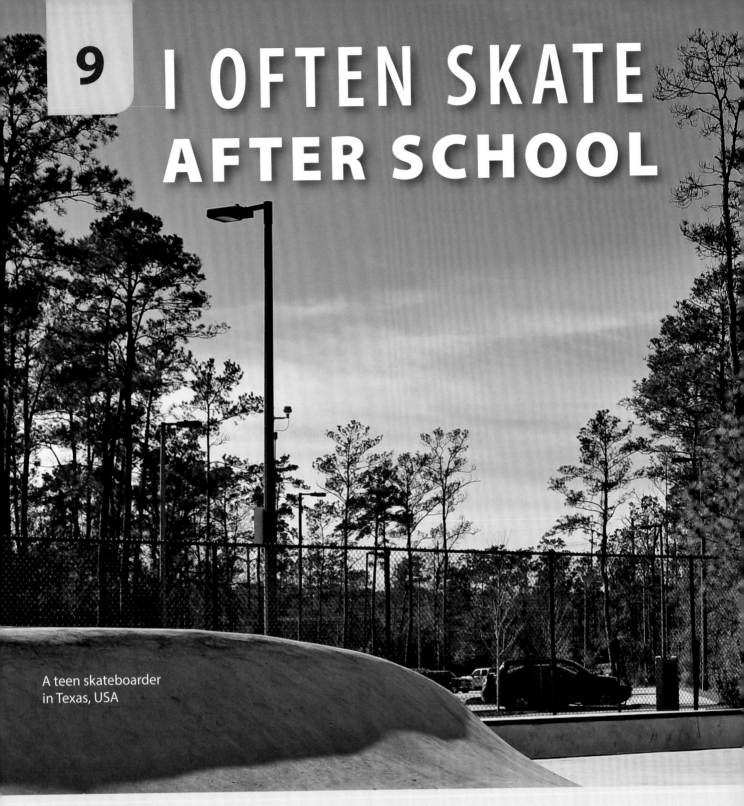

9 I OFTEN SKATE AFTER SCHOOL

A teen skateboarder in Texas, USA

PREVIEW

A 🎧 9.1 **Listen.** What is each person doing? Match.

1	Dan	○ ── ○ running	○ ── ○ after school
2	Ben	○ ── ○ cooking	○ ── ○ on Thursdays
3	Luis	○ ── ○ skating	○ ── ○ twice a week
4	Susana	○ ── ○ working	○ ── ○ every evening
5	Tim	○ ── ○ practicing the violin	○ ── ○ every day

B 🎧 9.1 **Listen again.** Match the activities in **A** to when th people usually do them.

PEOPLE AND PLACES

Talk with a partner. What do you do after school?

> I have dance practice after school on Mondays.

> I skate in the park every week.

UNIT GOALS

- talk about activities you are doing now
- use language for talking about how often you do something
- describe how habits form

103

LANGUAGE FOCUS

A 🎧 **9.2 Listen and read.** What does Stig do after school every day? Then repeat the conversation and replace the words in **bold**.

Stig: Hey, what do you usually do after school? Let's hang out sometime.

Ming: Sure. I **hardly ever** have activities after school. How about today? (**rarely / don't often**)

Stig: Uh, I can't. I **go to soccer practice** twice a week on Mondays and Thursdays. (**practice the piano / exercise**)

Ming: How about **tomorrow**? (**Wednesday / Friday**)

Stig: Actually, I go to **band practice** on Tuesdays, Wednesdays, and Fridays. (**art class / swimming lessons**)

Ming: So when *can* you hang out after school?

Stig: Hmm … Good question. How about Sunday?

B 🎧 **9.3 Look at the chart.** Then match the parts of the sentences below.

DESCRIBING ACTIVITIES (USING SIMPLE PRESENT AND PRESENT PROGRESSIVE)			
What are you **doing?**	I'm **reading** a magazine.		
Is she **cleaning** her room?	Yes, she **is**. / No, she **isn't**.		
What do you **do** after school?	I **play** soccer **every day**.		
	I play video games **once in a while**.		
Do you often **go** to the movies?	No, I	**rarely**	**go** to the movies.
		hardly ever	

1 We use the present progressive ○ (e.g., *writing*) to talk about   ○ actions that happen regularly.

2 We use the simple present ○ (e.g., *write*) to talk about   ○ actions that rarely happen.

3 We use *hardly ever* to talk about ○   ○ actions that are happening now.

104 Unit 9

C Circle the correct answers.

1 Dylan **listens** / **is listening** to music right now.

2 Alice **chats** / **is chatting** online every day.

3 Min **studies** / **is studying** for a test tomorrow.

4 They **practice** / **are practicing** the violin on Saturday mornings.

5 Joe **plays** / **is playing** soccer with his friends after school on Wednesdays.

D 🎧 9.4 Complete the conversations. Use the correct form of the words given. Then listen and check your answers.

1 **A:** What are you doing now?

   B: I _____ (**practice**) the violin.

2 **A:** Are you _____ (**study**) for a test?

   B: No, I'm not. I'm reading a magazine.

3 **A:** Do you _____ (**go**) to the café every week?

   B: Yes, I do.

4 **A:** What do you do after school?

   B: I usually _____ (**skate**) in the park.

E Work in a group. Play a game. On a piece of paper, write sentences about five activities you do. Place the papers face down. Choose a paper and read the sentences to the group. Guess who the sentences describe. Take turns.

I walk to school every day.

I often ride a scooter to the mall.

I play the piano once a week.

I hardly ever exercise.

I read magazines once in a while.

"I walk to school every day. I often ride a scooter …" Is this you, Jenny?

Sorry, it's not me!

THE REAL WORLD

THE SCIENCE OF HABITS

A teenager works in a quiet space to develop good study habits.

A ▶ 9.1 **Watch the video.** Match to complete the sentences.

1 A cue ○   ○ is something positive you get from a habit.
2 A routine ○   ○ causes a habit to happen.
3 A reward ○   ○ is the habit itself.

B ▶ 9.1 **Watch again.** Circle the correct words.

1 In the video, the first woman says she has a habit of **biting her nails** / **watching too much TV**.

2 In the video, the second woman has a bad habit of eating too much **salty** / **sweet** food.

3 Good habits help to create space in our brain so that we can think about **how to get to school** / **creative ideas**.

C **Read the sentences below.** Write *cue*, *routine*, or *reward*.

1 The sweet taste of candy   _____

2 Buying and eating candy   _____

3 Walking past a snack shop on the way to school   _____

D CRITICAL THINKING Evaluating **Discuss with a partner.** State one habit you have. Is it a good habit or a bad habit? How is it good or bad?

PROJECT Make a plan. What bad habit would you like to break? Identify the habit's cue, routine, and reward. What steps can you take to break this habit?

PRONUNCIATION homophones

🎧 **9.5** **Listen.** Circle the words you hear. Make sentences using one of the words in each pair and read them to a partner.

1	hear	here	**4**	I	eye
2	know	no	**5**	wear	where
3	too	two	**6**	for	four

IDIOM

"Old habits die hard" means it's _____ to change your habits.
a good
b difficult
c scary

COMMUNICATION

Find out about your classmates' habits. Work in a group. Talk about the habits below. Ask follow-up questions. Who do you think has the best habits in your group?

Do you ... ?	
• exercise	• help with housework
• arrive at school on time	• brush your teeth after eating
• clean your room	• eat healthy meals
• get enough sleep	• save money
• visit the dentist twice a year	• finish your homework early

Do you exercise?

Yes, I do.

How often do you exercise?

READING

A **Look at the title and photos.** What adjectives can you use to describe these children's commutes to school?

B **Scan the article.** What caused the bridge in Banten to break?

C **Talk with a partner.** How do you get to school?

A child rides a zip line across the Rio Negro Valley in Colombia.

UNUSUAL
COMMUTES

🎧 **9.6** How do you get to school? Do you usually go by bus, by car, or on foot? Some children have very unusual commutes to school.

Eleven families with children live on one side of the
5 Rio Negro Valley in Colombia. The children's **daily** commute is breathtaking. They **ride** a zip line 400 meters above the valley to get to the other side. It's the quickest way to get to school, but when it rains, the cable is too dangerous. The children stay
10 home and can't go to school.

Children from the village of Banten in Indonesia **cross** a river to get to school every day. In the past, the children crossed a **bridge,** but it broke after a heavy rain. The bridge was **broken** for 10 months.
15 There was another bridge they could use, but the journey was 30 minutes longer. Students usually **chose** to cross the broken bridge.

According to UNESCO, more than 63 million children around the world can't go to school. It's not
20 easy to solve this problem, but it's something we should continue to work on.

Children cross a broken bridge in Banten, Indonesia.

COMPREHENSION

A Answer the questions about *Unusual Commutes*.

1 MAIN IDEA The article is mainly about _____ ways children around the world travel to school.

    a interesting   **b** expensive   **c** relaxing

2 PURPOSE Why does the author write about the height of the zip line?

    a to explain why the commute is breathtaking

    b to explain why the children enjoy riding the zip line

    c to explain why the children spend hours to get to school

3 INFERENCE Why did the children in Banten use the broken bridge instead of the other one?

    a The other bridge was for cars.

    b They wanted to save time.

    c The other bridge was more dangerous.

4 DETAIL More than 63 million children around the world _____.

    a do not go to school

    b have unusual commutes to school

    c travel long distances to get to school

5 REFERENCE In line 20, *this problem* refers to _____.

    a the broken bridge

    b unusual commutes to school

    c children not being able to go to school

B Complete the notes. Choose one or two words from the article for each answer.

Common commutes to school • by bus, by car, or on [1] _____	
In Colombia • Some children ride a(n) [2] _____ to get across the Rio Negro Valley. • It can be dangerous to ride the zip line when it [3] _____.	**In Indonesia** • Children from Banten had to cross a broken [4] _____. • It was broken for 10 [5] _____.

C CRITICAL THINKING Analyzing Talk with a partner. Why do you think many children can't go to school?

VOCABULARY

A **Find the words below in the article.** Then complete the sentences with the correct form of the words in the box.

daily	ride	cross	bridge	broken	choose

1 Paula _____ a bicycle to school every day.

2 Practicing the violin is part of Jun's _____ routine.

3 The window was _____ because someone threw a rock at it.

4 Carl always _____ to take the bus instead of walking.

5 Every day, people _____ the _____ to the other side of the river.

B **Read the information below.** Then circle the correct answers.

> Here are some verbs to talk about travel.
> *get on*: board a train, bus, etc.
> *get off*: leave a train, bus, etc.
> *pick up*: collect someone or something from a place
> *take*: go somewhere by train, bus, etc.
> *take off*: leave the ground and begin to fly

1 Lucas **gets off** / **takes** the train to school every day.

2 Ana's parents **pick** / **get** her up from school every day.

3 Sofia **got off** / **took** at the wrong bus stop.

4 They **took off** / **got on** the train just before it left.

5 The plane to Paris **got** / **took off** three hours ago.

WRITING

A **Read the paragraph.**

B **Think about your school commute.** Make notes. How do you usually travel to school? What time do you usually leave your house? Add any other information.

C **Write a paragraph to describe your school commute.** Use your notes from **B**.

I usually bike to school. Sometimes, I walk. I leave my house every morning at 7.30 a.m. I usually reach school at around 8 a.m. I'm rarely late for school ...

HELPING **CHILDREN** TO **LOVE NATURE**

Before You Watch

Talk with a partner. Do you think it's important for children to learn about the environment? Why?

While You Watch

A 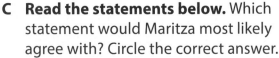 **9.2 Watch the video.** What are the children doing? Check the two (✓) correct answers.

◻ reading ◻ playing games ◻ growing plants ◻ feeding animals

B ▶ 9.2 **Watch again.** Read the sentences below. Circle the correct answers.

1 Maritza trains children to be **environmental teachers** / **engineers**.

2 The park uses **videos** / **games** to teach children.

3 Students do experiments **inside** / **outside**.

4 Teachers at the park are **children** / **adults**.

C Read the statements below. Which statement would Maritza most likely agree with? Circle the correct answer.

a Students learn best in a classroom.

b Students around the world should learn about the environment.

c Parents should help their children with their homework.

After You Watch

Talk with a partner. What kind of games or experiments do you think can help children learn about the environment?

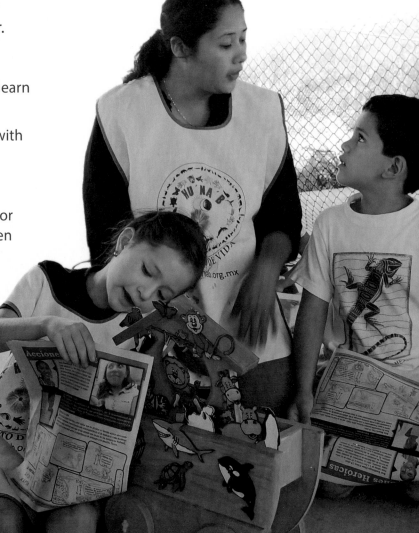

Maritza teaches children at her environmental theme park.

A Complete the sentences. Circle the correct answers.

Frank skates in the park ¹ **every day / twice a week**, on Mondays and Fridays. He ² **rides / crosses** the bus to get to the park. ³ **Hardly ever / Once in a while**, he goes to an ice cream shop after skating. To get there, he needs to ⁴ **cross / go** a busy road. At the shop, he ⁵ **practices / chooses** his favorite ice cream.

B Complete the conversation. Write the correct form of the verbs.

Sho: Hey Mari, what are you ¹ _____ (**do**)?

Mari: I'm ² _____ (**paint**). I always ³ _____ (**paint**) after school on Fridays. How about you?

Sho: I'm ⁴ _____ (**watch**) TV. I usually ⁵ _____ (**watch**) my favorite TV show on Friday evenings.

Mari: Oh, then what do you usually do on weekends?

Sho: I usually ⁶ _____ (**go**) to the beach.

Mari: That's nice! I hardly ever ⁷ _____ (**go**) to the beach. I usually ⁸ _____ (**practice**) the piano on Saturdays and ⁹ _____ (**hang**) out with my friends at the mall on Sundays.

C Complete the sentences. Circle the correct answers.

1 Harry is **getting / picking** his children **on / up** from the museum.

2 Paulo is **taking / getting off** a bus to the mall.

3 You should arrive at the airport two hours before your plane **takes off / gets on**.

4 The children are **picking up / getting off** the train.

5 You need to buy a ticket before you **take off / get on** the bus.

> **SELF CHECK**   Now I can …
>
> ◯ talk about activities I am doing now
>
> ◯ use language for talking about how often I do something
>
> ◯ describe how habits form

10 HOW DO YOU GET TO THE RESTAURANT?

Amagertorv in Copenhagen, Denmark

PREVIEW

A **10.1** **Listen.** Number the places (1–6) in the order you hear them.

Conversation 1

movie theater _____

restaurant _____

convenience store _____

Conversation 2

supermarket _____

museum _____

park _____

B **10.1** **Listen again.** Circle the correct answers.

1 There's a **convenience store** / **museum** next to the restaurant.

2 The movie theater is near **a supermarket** / **Akemi's house**.

3 The museum is next to a **movie theater**/ **park**.

4 There's a **supermarket** / **restaurant** across from the park.

C **Talk with a partner.** What places in your city do you like to go to?

> I often go to the café to read comics.

PEOPLE AND PLACES

UNIT GOALS

• give and ask for directions

• learn language for describing locations

• learn about how cities grow

LANGUAGE FOCUS

A 🎧 **10.2 Listen and read.** Where does Ming want to go? Then repeat the conversation and replace the words in **bold**.

Ming:	Excuse me, can you tell me how to get to **the art museum?** (**this mall / the movie theater**)
Person A:	Sure, no problem. It's on **Hill Street**, across from the square. (**Main Street / Second Avenue**)
Ming:	OK, thanks.
Ming:	Uh … excuse me, how do you get to the **art museum?** (**mall/ movie theater**)
Person B:	Go straight down Hill Street. It's on the corner of **West Avenue**. (**Main Street / King Street**)
Ming:	Hi, I'm looking for this place …
Person C:	That's easy! **It's right behind you!** (**You're right in front of it / You're right next to it**)

B 🎧 **10.3 Look at the chart.** Circle the correct answers below.

GIVING DIRECTIONS (USING PREPOSITIONS OF PLACE AND THE IMPERATIVE)		
Where's the museum?	It's	**behind / in front of** the supermarket.
		across from / next to the movie theater.
		between the mall **and** the park.
		on the corner of First Street **and** Main Avenue.
How do I **get to** the park?		**Go straight down** Main Street.
		Go past the hospital.
		Turn left / Make a right on First Avenue.

1 We use the imperative (e.g., *Turn left.*) to tell someone **where something is / what to do**.

2 When we use the imperative, we use the **base verb (e.g., *go*) / simple past (e.g., *went*)**.

3 In a sentence, the preposition (e.g., *next to*) usually comes **before / after** a place (e.g., *the park*).

C Look at the map below. Circle the correct answers.

1 The library is **across from** / **next to** the hospital.

2 The convenience store is **next to** / **in front of** the hotel.

3 There's a parking lot **between** / **on the corner of** the restaurant and the café.

4 The mall is **between** / **on the corner of** West Street and Broad Avenue.

D 🎧 10.4 Look again at the map. Number the directions (1–4) in the correct order. Then listen and check your answers.

1 Maya is at the zoo. How does she get to the train station?

a _____ Go past the pizza restaurant.

b _____ Turn right on Park Avenue.

c _____ Make a left on Riverside Street.

d __1__ Make a right and go straight down West Street.

2 I'm at Greenwood Park. How do I get to Valley Hospital?

a _____ Turn right on West Street.

b _____ It's on the left.

c _____ Make a left on Broad Avenue.

d __1__ Turn left and go straight down Riverside Street.

E Work with a partner. Play a guessing game. Take turns giving directions to a place in your school. Your partner guesses the place.

Go out of the classroom and turn left. Go straight down the hall. Turn right at the library. Go past the science lab. This place is on the left.

Is it the cafeteria?

THE REAL WORLD

A RIDE TO BUCKINGHAM PALACE

Buckingham Palace
in London, England

A ▶ 10.1 **Watch Part 1 of the video.** Circle the correct directions.

Turn ¹ **right** / **left** on Bloomsbury Way. Make a ² **right** / **left** onto Kingsway. Make a ³ **right** / **left** on Aldwych. Turn ⁴ **right** / **left** onto the Strand. At Trafalgar Square, take the ⁵ **first** / **third** exit onto the Mall.

B ▶ 10.2 **Close your books.** Watch **Part 2** of the video. Check your answers in **A**. How many did you get right?

C **Look at the map on page 119.** How do you get from Buckingham Palace to Westminster Abbey? Number the directions (1–5) in the correct order.

a _____ From Buckingham Palace, walk to Spur Road.

b _____ Westminster Abbey is right in front of you.

c _____ Make a left onto Birdcage Walk.

d _____ Cross Broad Sanctuary.

e _____ Turn right onto Storey's Gate.

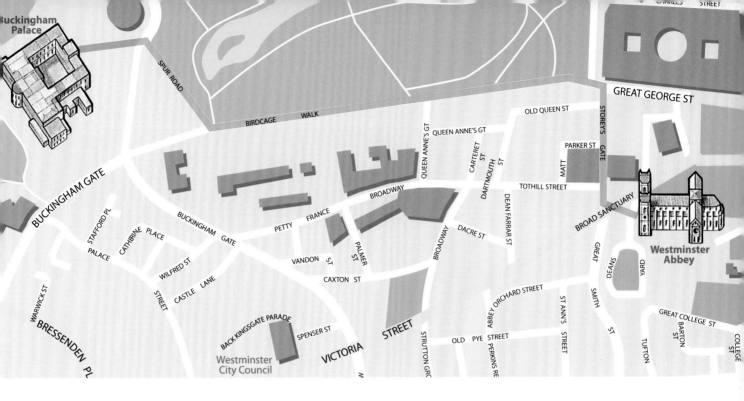

D CRITICAL THINKING Evaluating **Talk with a partner.** Besides using street names, some people give directions using landmarks, such as buildings. Which way do you prefer? Why?

PROJECT Write a walking tour of your neighborhood or city. Think of interesting places. Draw a map and mark their locations. Write directions to get from one place to the other.

PRONUNCIATION *o* sounds

🎧 10.5 **Complete the chart.** Listen and check your answers. Then read the words to a partner.

~~do~~   shoe   no   open   come   two   L<u>o</u>ndon   road

Sounds like *o* in movie	Sounds like *o* in go	Sounds like *o* in front
do		

COMMUNICATION

Work with a partner. Find the places. **Student A:** Turn to page 153 and follow the instructions. **Student B:** Turn to page 154 and follow the instructions.

How do I get to the café?

Turn right onto Fourth Avenue, then …

READING

A Skim the article. Wayfinding refers to the process of
_____ .

  a creating phone maps
  b discovering interesting places
  c knowing where we are and getting directions

B Scan the article. Which two apps are mentioned by name? Underline them.

C Talk with a partner. Describe a time when you got lost. How did you find your way again?

WAYFINDING
TECHNOLOGY

A tourist in New York City uses augmented reality (AR) to get directions.

A 🎧 **10.6** Phones are replacing maps as the best way to get directions from one place to another. You can type or even speak into your phone and **immediately** find your way. But even with these directions, it sometimes takes time to decide which way to go. This is especially true if you don't already know which street you are on.

B A new technology uses augmented reality (AR) to give directions through your phone's camera. When you hold up your phone, direction **signs** and street names pop up on the screen. Now, you know immediately if you need to turn right or left. It can also help you to remember where you **parked** your car.

C There are many apps to help you find your way. But some can do much more than that. For example, on the Waze app, people share information such as **traffic**, accidents, and road construction. If the traffic is bad, the app can **offer** different routes to help save time.

D Some apps can make your trip more enjoyable. For example, an app called Geotourist offers audio guides to tell you about interesting places around you. You can also create your own **tour** and share your photos.

E Wayfinding technology is making it easier for us to get directions. Maybe you could download an app this weekend and compare it to a paper map: which one do you think is better?

COMPREHENSION

DO YOU KNOW?

The world's longest walking route is from South Africa to _____.

a Russia
b Italy

A Answer the questions about *Wayfinding Technology*.

1 MAIN IDEA The article is mainly about how technology _____.

   a helps us to find our way

   b makes trips interesting

   c gives information about things around us

2 DETAIL When using augmented reality, you need to hold up your phone so it can _____.

   a identify the street you are on

   b share your location with your friends

   c take photos of places around you

3 REFERENCE The word *that* in the second sentence of paragraph C refers to _____.

   a augmented reality   b a wayfinding app   c providing directions

4 INFERENCE The Waze app is most useful for people who are _____.

   a walking   b driving   c exploring a new place

5 DETAIL The Geotourist app has all of the following EXCEPT _____.

   a audio guides

   b photos of interesting places

   c information about road accidents

B Match the sentences to the technology. Write the letters (**a–d**) next to the correct names (**1–3**).

   a It helps you to avoid heavy traffic.
   b It allows you to create your own tours.
   c It uses your phone camera to show directions.
   d It allows you to share information about traffic.

1 augmented reality   _____

2 Waze   _____

3 Geotourist   _____

C CRITICAL THINKING Analyzing Talk with a partner. Why do you think some people still use paper maps?

VOCABULARY

A **Find the words below in the article.** Then match them to their meanings.

1 immediately ○   ○ leave a car somewhere

2 sign ○   ○ give something

3 park ○   ○ without waiting

4 traffic ○   ○ a visit to or around a place

5 offer ○   ○ vehicles moving on a road

6 tour ○   ○ a notice that gives you instructions or information

IDIOM

"A step in the right direction" is an action that _____ .
a helps you get what you want
b gets you in trouble

B **Read the information below.** Then complete the sentences with the linking words.

> We use linking words such as *finally*, *first*, and *then* to describe the sequence of events.

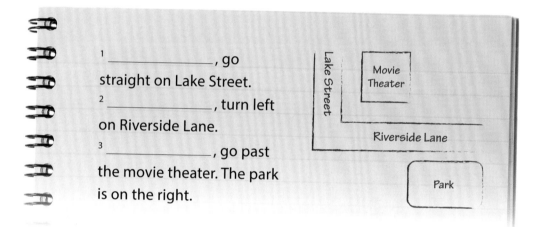

1 _____, go straight on Lake Street.
2 _____, turn left on Riverside Lane.
3 _____, go past the movie theater. The park is on the right.

Lake Street | Movie Theater | Riverside Lane | Park

WRITING

A **Imagine your friends are going to your house for a party.** Look at a map. Make notes. What's the best way for your friends to find your house?

B **Read the text message.**

C **Write a text message.** Give directions to help your friends get to your house. Use your notes from **A**.

5:15 PM

N
Nancy

Hi, my house is on the corner of Main Street and Second Avenue. If you are coming here by bus, get off at the bus stop across from the supermarket. Then go straight on First Avenue and make a left on …

Delivered

SHAPE OF **CITIES**

Before You Watch

Talk with a partner. What do you know about the history of your city?

While You Watch

A ▶ 10.3 **Watch the video.** Look at Maps 1–3. Match the maps to the cities.

| Map 1 | Map 2 | Map 3 |

Shanghai _____   Manila _____   Lagos _____

B ▶ 10.3 **Watch again.** Circle **T** for True or **F** for False.

1   The population of Shanghai today is about ten
    times its population in 1982.   **T**   **F**

2   Manila grew in an east-west direction.   **T**   **F**

3   Lagos has many areas covered with shallow water.   **T**   **F**

C   **Match the cities to the correct descriptions.**

   Shanghai   Manila   Lagos

1   This city is between the sea and a lake.   _____

2   This city grew when the country started   _____
    producing a lot of oil.

3   This city grew when its country opened   _____
    up to businesses from other countries.

After You Watch

Talk with a partner. Think about your city. How is it different
today than in the past?

A **Complete the sentences.** Use the words in the box.

> immediately   traffic   between   park   corner

1 We should leave the house early to avoid the morning _____ .

2 The convenience store is on the _____ of Hill Street and Second Avenue.

3 The Italian restaurant is _____ the supermarket and the art museum.

4 You can _____ at the side of the road.

5 Sonia is hurt—we should take her to the hospital _____ .

B **Write the sentences.** Use the words given.

1 straight / go / Lake Street / down

_____ .

2 the / supermarket / where's

_____ ?

3 get / how / I / do / the / to / movie theater

_____ ?

4 between / the museum / the pizza restaurant / it's / and

_____ .

C **Complete the conversation.** Circle the correct answers.

A: Excuse me, can you tell me how to get to the nearest convenience store?

B: Sure. [1] **First / Finally,** go straight down this street. [2] **Then / First,** turn left and go down Riverside Street. [3] **Finally / First,** walk past the Mexican restaurant. The convenience store is on the right.

SELF CHECK Now I can ...

☐ give and ask for directions

☐ use language for describing locations

☐ talk about how cities grow

Manila, capital city of the Philippines

WHAT WERE
YOU DOING?

A BASE jumper jumps off Angel Falls in Venezuela.

PREVIEW

A 🎧 **11.1 Listen to Part 1 of the conversation.** Circle the correct answers.

BASE jumping is ¹ **an adventure sport / a competition**. People jump from places like ² **planes / buildings** and mountains. They wear special suits called ³ **skysuits / wingsuits**. These help them to fly.

B 🎧 **11.2 Listen to Part 2 of the conversation.** Circle **T** for True or **F** for False.

1 Rachel felt nervous when she was watching the people jump.   **T   F**

2 You need to have skydiving experience to do BASE jumping.   **T   F**

3 The skills for skydiving and BASE jumping are very different.   **T   F**

4 In the future, Rachel wants to do BASE jumping.   **T   F**

C Talk with a partner. Have you ever tried something risky? What did you do?

> I tried mountain biking for the first time.

> I went bungee jumping.

SCIENCE AND TECHNOLOGY

UNIT GOALS

• describe your past experiences

• use language for showing the order of two past events

• learn about a special kind of memory

LANGUAGE FOCUS

A 🎧 **11.3 Listen and read.** Why didn't Maya wake up on time? Then repeat the conversation and replace the words in **bold**.

Ming: Hey, where are you? The movie starts in 15 minutes! Hurry up!

Maya: Sorry, I **forgot to set my alarm**! I'm leaving the house now. (**slept in / just woke up**)

Ming: Why didn't you set your alarm?

Maya: I was tired. I was **reading a book** when I fell asleep. (**watching TV / listening to music**)

Ming: Why were you so tired?

Maya: I was **playing with** my younger cousins yesterday. (**taking care of / babysitting**)

Maya: And here I am!

Ming: Um, Maya, you're still wearing pajamas!

B 🎧 **11.4 Look at the chart.** Circle the correct answers below.

DESCRIBING ORDER OF EVENTS (USING SIMPLE PAST AND PAST PROGRESSIVE)	
I **was skateboarding when** I **fell**. She **was cleaning** her room **when** I **came** home. We **were playing** soccer **when** the rain **started**.	
Were you **eating** when she **called**? What **were** you **doing** at 8 o'clock last night?	Yes, I **was**. / No, I **wasn't**. I **was studying**.

1 We use the **simple past / past progressive** to describe a completed action.

2 We use the **simple past / past progressive** to describe a continuing action in the past.

3 When telling a story, we use the **simple past / past progressive** for the action that started first. We use the **simple past / past progressive** for the event that happened second.

C 🎧 **11.5 Complete the sentences.** Use the words in parentheses to help you. Then listen and check.

1 He _____ (**do**) his homework when you _____ (**call**).

2 They _____ (**see**) an accident while they _____ (**drive**) home from school.

3 I _____ (**bike**) when I _____ (**meet**) a friend.

4 I _____ (**find**) a lost dog while I _____ (**walk**) in the park.

5 We _____ (**climb**) a mountain when my brother _____ (**hurt**) his knee.

D Complete the sentences. Write your own ideas.

1 I was talking on the phone when _____ .

2 I was _____ when the bell rang.

3 She was skateboarding when _____ .

4 They _____ when the fire started.

5 We _____ when we heard music.

6 I was practicing the piano when _____ .

E Work in a group. Create a story. Take turns adding a sentence. Make your story as long as possible.

> I was eating dinner when I heard a knock on the door.

> The cat was digging a hole near a tree.

> When I opened the door, I saw a cat.

FLASHBULB MEMORY

A family watches a live television broadcast of the first Moon landing in 1969.

A **Talk with a partner.** What's an important experience that you can remember? What do you remember about it?

B ▶ 11.1 **Watch the video.** Check (✓) the two correct answers. Which of the following will most likely become flashbulb memories?

- ☐ going to school by bus
- ☐ getting a surprise birthday party
- ☐ having pizza for dinner
- ☐ falling down a steep hill

DO YOU KNOW?

Most people can't remember things from before they were _____ years old.
a three
b seven

C ▶ 11.1 **Watch again. Circle T for True or F for False.**

1 Flashbulb memories got their name from the way people took photographs in the past.   **T**   **F**

2 Flashbulb memories usually contain only the main details of an event.   **T**   **F**

3 Flashbulb memories are more accurate than ordinary memories.   **T**   **F**

D [CRITICAL THINKING Reflecting] **Talk with a partner.** Why do you think flashbulb memories seem more accurate than ordinary memories?

> **PROJECT Do a survey.** Ask older family members about flashbulb moments in their lives. Find two people with a memory of the same event. Compare their memories. How are they different?

PRONUNCIATION ending blends: *-sk, -st, -nk, -nt*

A 🎧 11.6 **Listen.** Circle the sounds you hear.

1	nt	nk		2	st	sk		3	sk	st
4	nk	nt		5	sk	st		6	nt	nk

B **Work with a partner.** Take turns reading the words in the box.

> task   thank   past   accident   risk   think

COMMUNICATION

Work in pairs. Look at the pictures below. Pick one action from each column. Make a sentence using these two actions. Read them to a partner. Ask follow-up questions.

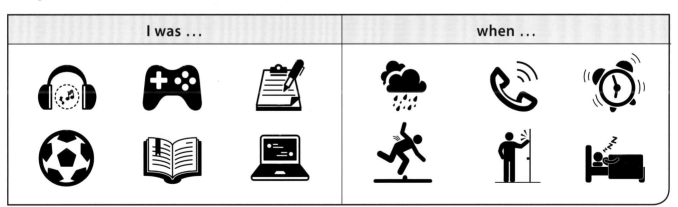

I was playing soccer when the rain started.

What did you do after that?

DIVING WITH SHARKS

READING

A **Skim the article.** We know that Amanda loves sharks because _____ .
a   she went diving in the ocean
b   she shared the photo of a shark online
c   she teaches her class about protecting sharks

B **Scan the article.** How does Amanda describe sharks?

C **Talk with a partner.** What do you think of sharks? Use adjectives to describe them.

A diver films a great white shark in Australia.

🎧 **11.7** Amanda Brewer is a teacher from New Jersey in the United States. She is very **interested** in sharks. She even traveled to South Africa as a volunteer for White Shark
5 Africa, a company that works to protect sharks.

In the summer of 2014, Amanda was volunteering in Mossel Bay, South Africa. She was working with scientists on a project to collect information about sharks. She was also
10 helping out on shark-watching trips.

On one of these trips, Amanda went diving in the ocean inside a metal cage. She was **hoping** to see a shark. She didn't have to **wait** very long. A great white shark appeared and swam
15 straight toward the cage. It was very **close**. It wanted to eat a piece of meat tied to the cage. Amanda took a photo of the animal just when it opened its mouth.

Amanda was very **excited** about her experience
20 with the shark—she said she wasn't **afraid** at all. "They're beautiful, powerful, and intelligent, and it erases all the fear," she explained. After her experience, she shared her photo online and it went viral.

25 Her picture appeared in newspapers and on websites around the world. She also hung the photo in her classroom for her students to see. She uses it to teach her students that we should protect sharks.

COMPREHENSION

A Answer the questions about *Diving with Sharks*.

1 **MAIN IDEA** The article is mainly about _____ .

   a a shark attack

   b dangerous sharks

   c getting close to a shark

2 **DETAIL** Which of the following is NOT true about Amanda?

   a She is a teacher.

   b She is a full-time scientist.

   c She was a volunteer for White Shark Africa.

3 **INFERENCE** The shark swam to the cage because it was _____ .

   a angry   **b** hungry   **c** playful

4 **VOCABULARY** In line 24, *it went viral* means many people _____ the photo.

   a shared   **b** bought   **c** commented on

5 **PURPOSE** Why does the author mention that Amanda's photo appeared in newspapers and on websites?

   a to show how amazing Amanda's photo is

   b to show that Amanda saw a rare animal

   c to show that many people love sharks

> **IDIOM**
>
> "It was a close shave" means that something _____ almost happened.
> **a** amazing
> **b** dangerous

B Complete the chart. Write notes to describe Amanda's experience.

Where did it happen?	In Mossel Bay, [1] _____
Why did she go there?	She was volunteering for [2] _____ .
When did it happen?	In the [3] _____ of 2014
What happened?	She saw a(n) [4] _____ when she was [5] _____ .

C **CRITICAL THINKING Analyzing** **Look at the article.** Identify two facts and two opinions. Then discuss your ideas with a partner.

VOCABULARY

A Find the words below in the article. Then complete the sentences using the words in the box.

> interested   hope   wait   close   excited   afraid

New message   _ ☐ ✕

Hi Carlos,

How did you spend your holiday? My family and I went on a trip to the beach. My brother taught me how to surf—he's very ¹ _____ in surfing. I fell into the water many times. At first, I was ² _____ of getting ³ _____ to the huge waves. But now, I'm so ⁴ _____ to surf again! I can't ⁵ _____ to tell you more. I ⁶ _____ to see you soon!

Best regards,

Martin

Send   A 🔗 😃 ∞ 🖼   🗑 ☰

B Read the information below. Then match the words in **bold** to their meanings.

> Homonyms are words that have the same spelling but different meanings.
>
> **share** *(verb)* **1.** divide something between two or more people; **2.** have the same feelings or ideas
>
> **straight** *(adverb)* **1.** immediately; **2.** in a straight line

1 They **share** an interest in sports. ○
2 Zoe **shared** a pizza with her friends. ○
3 Go **straight** and turn left on Main Street. ○
4 I went **straight** home from school yesterday. ○

○ immediately
○ have the same feelings or ideas
○ in a line
○ divide something between two or more people

WRITING

A Read the paragraph.

B Think about a time you came close to an animal. Make notes. What happened? Add any other information.

C Describe your experience. Use your notes from **B**.

When I was a kid, I saw some parrots at the zoo. I was feeding them when one of them landed on my hand. I was so afraid ...

THE *MISINFORMATION* EFFECT

Before You Watch

Talk with a partner. Do you think you have a good memory? What things can you remember well?

While You Watch

A ▶ 11.2 **Watch Part 1 of the video.** What do you remember about the accident? Circle the correct answers.

The [1] **red / blue** car hit the [2] **side / back** of the [3] **red / blue** car. Then, it drove past a [4] **stop / yield** sign before it drove away.

B ▶ 11.3 **Watch Part 2 of the video.** Check your answers in **A**. Were you able to remember all the details correctly? Why or why not? Discuss with a partner.

C ▶ 11.3 **Watch Part 2 of the video again.** Circle **T** for True or **F** for False.

1   The misinformation effect shows that some of our memories can be wrong.   **T**   **F**

2   New information can change our memory of a past event.   **T**   **F**

3   We form the most accurate memories when we are under stress.   **T**   **F**

After You Watch

Talk with a partner. Think about your answers in **Before You Watch**. Do you still feel the same way about your memory?

A car on its side after an accident

A Complete the sentences. Use the words in the box.

accidents	experience	wait	excited

1 Please _____ for me at the bus stop.

2 The storm caused traffic _____ across the country.

3 Carl was very _____ to get a pet.

4 Maria wrote about her _____ of living in Africa.

B Complete the sentences. Circle the correct answers.

1 Sue **leave / left** the room while the band was practicing.

2 Amanda **is / was** diving when the shark **appeared / was appearing**.

3 **Ann:** What were you **do / doing** yesterday?
   Ian: I **skated / was skating** in the park.

C Match the words in bold to their meanings.

a immediately

b in a line

c have the same feelings or ideas

d divide something between two or more people

1 Eva forgot to bring her lunch, so I **shared** my sandwich   _____
   with her.

2 Juan and I **share** the same thoughts about the movie.   _____

3 The students placed the tables and chairs in   _____
   straight rows.

4 These cookies came **straight** from the oven.   _____

SELF CHECK   Now I can ...

☐ describe my past experiences

☐ use language for showing the order of two past events

☐ explain a special kind of memory

WE'RE GOING TO VOLUNTEER!

PREVIEW

A **Work with a partner.** Talk about the photo using the words in the box.

clean	trash	volunteer
beach	plastic	pick up

B 🎧 **12.1** **Listen.** Check (✓) the activities that Martha and Kathy are going to do.

- ☐ volunteer
- ☐ clean a beach
- ☐ put up decorations
- ☐ plan a charity event
- ☐ raise money
- ☐ guide visitors

Teens volunteer at an event in Cape Town, South Africa.

PEOPLE AND PLACES

UNIT GOALS

- describe your future plans
- use language for expressing future time
- learn about volunteer activities

Talk with a partner. Have you ever been a volunteer? What did you do?

I collected old newspapers for recycling.

I made cards to sell at my school fair.

LANGUAGE FOCUS

A 🎧 **12.2** **Listen and read.** What's Ming going to do for the charity dance? Then repeat the conversation and replace the words in **bold**.

Nadine: We're going to have the charity dance in the gym. Who's going to decorate it?

Ming: I am! I **made some awesome decorations**. (**made some cool posters** / **bought lots of balloons**)

Nadine: OK, we need music. Maya, are you going to be the DJ?

Maya: Definitely! I'm going to play some cool **hip-hop** music. (**rock** / **dance**)

Nadine: Who's going to bring the food?

Stig: I'm going to **bake some cookies**. Ming's going to help. (**make cupcakes** / **bake a cake**)

Ming: So, Nadine, what are you going to do?

Nadine: Well, I'm going to come to the dance and **eat the cookies**! (**have a great time** / **enjoy the music**)

B 🎧 **12.3** **Look at the chart.** Circle the correct answers below.

DESCRIBING FUTURE PLANS (USING *GOING TO* AND EXPRESSING FUTURE TIME)	
I'm **going to volunteer** at a school event. / She's **going to sing** at the party. / They're **going to collect** food waste.	
Are you **going to come** to the party?	Yes, **I am**. / No, **I'm not**.
What's he **going to do**? **What** are you **going to eat**?	He's **going to play** music. I'm **going to eat** a sandwich.
When are you **going to go** to the mall?	I'm **going to go** there **tomorrow** / **next week**.

1 We use *going to* to talk about _____. **a** past experiences   **b** future plans

2 We use *going to* + _____.   **a** base verb (e.g., *help*)   **b** simple past (e.g., *helped*)

3 We use adverbs of time (e.g., *tomorrow*) to tell us _____ something happens.
   a when   **b** how often

C Write questions for the answers. Use *going to* and the words in parentheses to help you.

1 _What's Matt going to do_ ? (**Matt / do**) He's going to make T-shirts.

2 _____ ? (**Kwan / volunteer**) Yes, he is.

3 _____ ? (**Mary / draw**) No, she isn't.

4 _____ ? (**Sofia / sing**) No, she's going to put up decorations.

5 _____ ? (**Lucas / do**) He's going to raise money for charity.

D 🎧 12.4 Complete the conversation. Use the correct form of the words in parentheses. Then listen and check your answers.

Marco: Hey Jia Li, are you going to go to the school dance?

Jia Li: ¹ Yes, _____ (**be**). What time does it start?

Marco: It starts at seven.

Jia Li: I can't wait! ² _____ are you ³ _____ ? (**wear**)

Marco: I don't have a suit, so I'm going to wear my brother's. What about you?

Jia Li: I'm ⁴ _____ (**wear**) the dress I bought recently.

Marco: Are you ⁵ _____ (**bring**) your friends to the dance? They said we could invite friends.

Jia Li: Yeah, I am. A few of my friends are ⁶ _____ . (**come**)

E Work in a group. Play a game. Think of an activity, such as playing soccer, going to school, or sleeping. Say the things you do to prepare for the activity. Your group members guess the activity that you are going to do. Take turns.

> I bring out my brushes. I mix different colors. What am I going to do?

> You're going to paint!

THE REAL WORLD

SCIENTISTS
FOR A DAY

Citizen scientists at a BioBlitz event

A **Read the definition below.** Then answer the question.

> **citizen scientist** *noun* a non-scientist volunteer who collects data and records observations

Which of the following are benefits of using citizen scientists? Check (✓) your answers.

☐ They may need training. ☐ They can help to collect large amounts of data.

☐ They work for free. ☐ The data they collect may not be accurate.

B ▶ 12.1 **Watch the video.** What animals did you see? Check (✓) the two correct answers.

 ☐ rat ☐ insect  ☐ frog ☐ monkey

C ▶ 12.1 **Watch again.** Circle **T** for True or **F** for False.

1 The goal of the event was to count the kinds of plants and animals in the park.   **T**   **F**

2 The volunteers finished before it got dark.   **T**   **F**

3 It was sunny throughout the event.   **T**   **F**

4 Volunteers shared photos of plants and animals online.   **T**   **F**

D CRITICAL THINKING Analyzing **Talk with a partner.** What kind of research do you think citizen scientists can help with?

PROJECT Work with a partner. Take photos of plants and animals in a park near you and identify them.

PRONUNCIATION reduction: *going to*

🎧 12.5 **Listen.** Complete the sentences. Then read the sentences to a partner.

1 We're _____ a school dance next week.

2 Are you _____ money for charity?

3 The DJ is _____ some awesome music.

4 Joe and Maria are _____ cookies and cupcakes.

5 Who's _____ posters for the dance?

COMMUNICATION

Plan a school charity sale. Work in a group of three. Take turns asking what your group members are going to do. Then complete the chart.

Student A: Look at the chart below.

Student B: Look at the chart on page 153.

Student C: Look at the chart on page 154.

When	Student A	Student B	Student C
today	design a T-shirt		
tomorrow	make decorations		
next week	buy plates and cups		
on the day of the sale	sell the drinks		

What are you going to do today?

I'm going to design a T-shirt.

READING

A **Scan the article.** What are the places that waste food? Underline them.

B **Look at the chart below the article.** Which of these statements is true? Circle the correct answer.
  a We waste a higher percentage of dairy products than meat.
  b We waste more than a third of the fish and seafood we produce.
  c We eat more than 60 percent of the fruits and vegetables we produce.

C **Talk with a partner.** Would you buy "ugly" food? Why or why not?

Very often, fruits and vegetables go to waste because they look ugly.

THE "UGLY" FOOD CHALLENGE

A 🎧 12.6 Tristram Stuart has 24 hours to **prepare** a meal for 5,000 people. He's going to plan a menu, gather food, cook, then **welcome** his guests. As part of the challenge, almost all of the ingredients must be from farms and stores that don't want them. This sounds like a TV show, but it's not—it's one of Tristram's campaigns to stop food waste.

B First, Tristram travels to a farm and collects vegetables that farmers think are too "ugly" to sell. Then, he stops at a farmers' market to collect vegetables that sellers threw away. Hours later, thousands of people enjoy the food his team of volunteers prepared.

C **Nearly** 800 million people around the world do not get enough food. But according to the United Nations, we **waste** enough food to feed every one of them. Why do we waste so much food? Stores and restaurants waste food when they **order** or **serve** too much. Supermarkets throw fresh fruit and vegetables away because they have strange shapes or colors. And at home, we often throw our leftovers away.

D Many people like Tristram are trying to stop food waste. For example, volunteers at Keep Austin Fed— an organization in Austin, Texas—save over 20,000 kilograms of food each month. Every day, they collect unwanted food from sellers and give it to people in need.

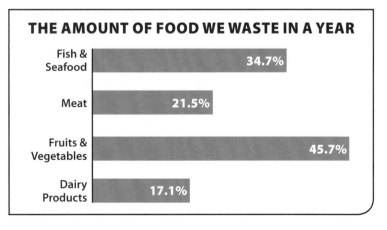

THE AMOUNT OF FOOD WE WASTE IN A YEAR

Fish & Seafood	34.7%
Meat	21.5%
Fruits & Vegetables	45.7%
Dairy Products	17.1%

COMPREHENSION

A **Answer the questions about** *The "Ugly" Food Challenge.*

1 **MAIN IDEA** This article is mainly about _____ .

   a why people don't buy "ugly" fruits and vegetables

   b how much food we waste

   c how people use unwanted food to feed others

2 **REFERENCE** The word *This* in the last sentence of paragraph A refers to _____ .

   a Tristram's challenge

   b Tristram's TV show

   c Tristram's team of volunteers

3 **DETAIL** Tristram collected food from all of the following EXCEPT _____ .

   a farms   **b** restaurants   **c** farmers' markets

4 **INFERENCE** Supermarkets throw away "ugly" food because they think _____ .

   a it tastes bad   **b** it goes bad quickly   **c** no one wants to buy it

5 **DETAIL** Volunteers at Keep Austin Fed _____ .

   a cook meals for hungry people

   b sell unwanted food at low prices

   c give unwanted food to hungry people

B **Match.** Which paragraph contains the following information?

1 the amount of food Keep Austin Fed saves each month ○	○ Paragraph A
2 the number of meals Tristram has to prepare ○	○ Paragraph B
3 where Tristram got food for the campaign ○	○ Paragraph C
3 the number of hungry people around the world ○	○ Paragraph D

C **CRITICAL THINKING Reflecting**

Talk with a partner. List three habits that can help you reduce food waste.

HOW TO REDUCE FOOD WASTE

VOCABULARY

A Find these words in the article. Then complete the sentences using the words in the box.

> prepare   welcome   nearly   waste   order   serve

1   The students put up decorations to _____ their new classmate from Japan.

2   A waiter's job is to _____ food to the customers.

3   Water is important to us—we should not _____ it.

4   Mia is _____ as tall as her mother.

5   Sofia is helping her daughter to _____ for her exams.

6   My parents are going to _____ food from their favorite restaurant.

B Read the information below. Then circle the correct answers.

> We use nouns to refer to different types of food.
> *dessert*: sweet food you eat at the end of a meal
> *ingredients*: food used to prepare a dish
> *leftovers*: extra food left at the end of a meal
> *main course*: the largest part of a meal

IDIOM

When you have "too much on your plate," you have _____.
a too much food
b a lot of work or problems

1   Mateo had pizza for his **dessert** / **main course**.

2   There were a lot of **leftovers** / **main courses** from the party.

3   The chef uses fresh **ingredients** / **leftovers**.

4   After the main course, I had ice cream for **ingredient** / **dessert**.

WRITING

A Read the beginning of the article about an event.

B Choose an event. Make notes. What's the event about? What are the volunteers going to do? Add other information.

C Write an article to get volunteers to join the event. Use your notes from **B**.

WE NEED YOU!

UGLY FOOD FEAST is an event that calls attention to food waste. We need 10 volunteers for the event. The volunteers are going to collect unwanted food from . . .

FEEDING THE 5,000

Before You Watch

Talk with a partner. Read the statements below. Check (✓) any that you think are true.

- [ ] Food waste can cause pollution.
- [ ] It's not safe to eat vegetables with spots on them.
- [ ] To feed all the hungry people in the world, we need to produce more food.

While You Watch

A ▶ 12.2 **Watch the video.** Circle the correct answers.

1 The United States throws away about **40** / **70** percent of the food it produces.

2 Dominika talks about people rejecting food because it **looks** / **tastes** bad.

3 The Feeding the 5,000 event is aimed at **pressuring big companies** / **raising individuals' awareness**.

B ▶ 12.2 **Watch again.** Circle **T** for True or **F** for False.

1 The volunteers prepared the food at home before bringing it to the event.   **T**   **F**

2 The volunteers served vegetable curry at the event.   **T**   **F**

3 The volunteers cooked and served the food on the same day.   **T**   **F**

C **Circle the correct answer.** When Tristram said, "it's time to take food waste off the menu," he means that _____.

a we should not buy fast food

b we should stop food waste

c restaurants should serve unwanted food

After You Watch

Talk with a partner. What can your school do to reduce food waste?

A man gets free food at a Feeding the 5,000 event.

A Complete the sentences. Circle the correct answers.

New message   _ □ ×

Hi Joe,

I'm planning an event to ¹ **raise** / **waste** money for an animal shelter. I have a team of ² **visitors** / **volunteers** to help me. Ben is going to ³ **serve** / **put up** decorations and Sofia is going to ⁴ **welcome** / **order** the guests. We need some volunteers to ⁵ **prepare** / **guide** the food. Do you want to join us?

Eva

Send   A 🖉 ☺ ∞ 🖼   🗑 ≡

B Write the sentences. Use the words given.

1 going / mall / do / are / what / you/ to / at / the

_____?

2 plan / to / she's / charity / going / event / a

_____.

3 beach / are / when / go to / the / going to / you

_____?

C Complete the sentences. Write *dessert, ingredient, leftovers,* or *main course.*

1 Max ate the _____ from last night's dinner.

2 The main _____ of this dish is fish.

3 She had chicken for the _____ . After that, she ordered a cake for _____ .

SELF CHECK Now I can …

☐ describe my future plans

☐ use language for expressing future time

☐ talk about volunteer activities

UNIT 1 COMMUNICATION

Student B: Share your schedule. Complete the schedule below. Don't show your partner. Ask and answer questions about your partner's schedule.

Time	Monday	Tuesday	Wednesday	Thursday	Friday
Before school					
Morning					
Lunch					
Afternoon					
After school					

UNIT 2 COMMUNICATION

Work with a partner. Student A: Choose one person in the photos. Don't tell your partner who it is.
Student B: Ask yes/no questions to guess your partner's choice. Take turns.

UNIT 4 COMMUNICATION

Student A: Play a quiz game. Work with a partner. Take turns asking and answering questions. The correct answers are in **bold**.

Questions
1 What's the highest mountain in Japan?   a Mount Kita   b **Mount Fuji**
2 What's the hottest desert in Africa?   a **the Sahara**   b the Taklimakan Desert
3 Which city has the most bridges?   a Seoul, South Korea   b **Hamburg, Germany**
4 What's the smallest country in Asia by area?   a Singapore   b **the Maldives**
5 What's the windiest city in the world?   a **Wellington, New Zealand**   b Chicago, USA
6 What's the coldest continent?   a Australia   b **Antarctica**
7 Which bird lays the largest eggs?   a **ostrich**   b emperor penguin
8 What's the largest country by area?   a **Russia**   b Canada

UNIT 7 COMMUNICATION

Student B: Find the differences. Look at the picture below. Take turns asking and answering questions to find seven differences. Circle them.

UNIT 4 COMMUNICATION

Student B: Play a quiz game. Work with a partner. Take turns asking and answering questions. The correct answers are in **bold**.

Questions
1 What's the oldest musical instrument?   a **the flute**   b the violin
2 Which city has the most fountains?   a **Rome, Italy**   b Paris, France
3 What's the highest mountain in Africa?   a Mount Kenya   b **Mount Kilimanjaro**
4 What's the largest desert in Asia?   a the Arabian Desert   b **the Gobi**
5 What's the biggest country in South America by area?   a Argentina   b **Brazil**
6 Which country has the most public holidays?   a **Cambodia**   b Finland
7 What's the heaviest land animal?   a **the African elephant**   b the hippopotamus
8 What's the largest ocean on Earth?   a **the Pacific Ocean**   b the Atlantic Ocean

UNIT 8 COMMUNICATION

Work in a group of four. Do a survey. First, check (✓) the healthy habits you follow. Then ask the other members of your group about their healthy habits. Discuss the results as a group. Talk about other things you can do to stay healthy.

Healthy Habits	Name			
	You			
1 I get plenty of sleep.				
2 I always wash my hands before I eat.				
3 I drink lots of water.				
4 I exercise most days.				
5 I get a flu vaccination every year.				

UNIT 10 COMMUNICATION

Student A: Find the places. Look at the map below. Take turns asking your partner for directions to each place and label them on your map. Then compare and check your maps.

mall   café   history museum   supermarket   school   pizza restaurant

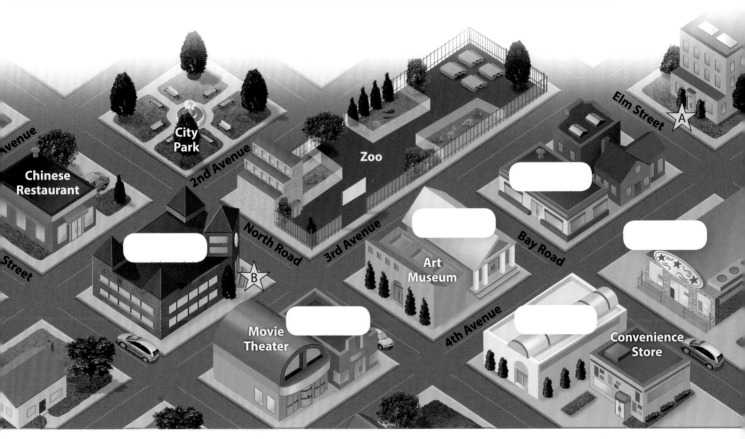

UNIT 12 COMMUNICATION

Student B: Plan a school charity sale. Take turns asking what your group members are going to do. Then complete the chart.

When	Student A	Student B	Student C
today		plan the games	
tomorrow		buy balloons	
next week		put up decorations	
on the day of the sale		make sandwiches	

UNIT 10 COMMUNICATION

Student B: Find the places. Look at the map below. Take turns asking your partner for directions to each place and label them on your map. Then compare and check your maps.

movie theater   art museum   convenience store   zoo   City Park   Chinese restaurant

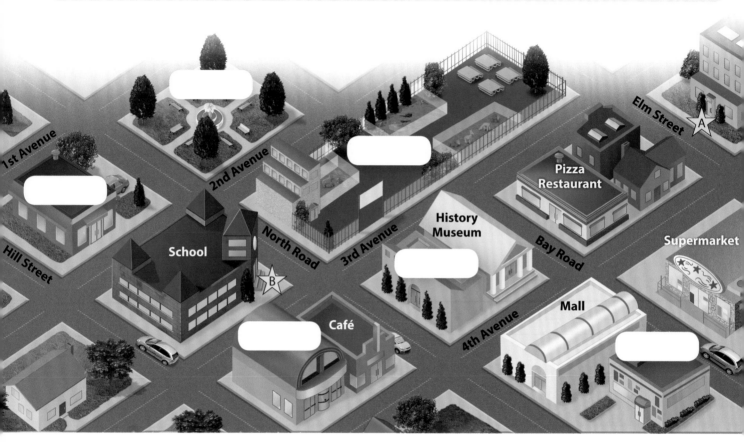

UNIT 12 COMMUNICATION

Student C: Plan a school charity sale. Take turns asking what your group members are going to do. Then complete the chart.

When	Student A	Student B	Student C
today			design the poster
tomorrow			make posters
next week			choose the music
on the day of the sale			sell sandwiches

IRREGULAR PAST TENSE VERBS

Base form	Past form
become	became
bring	brought
build	built
buy	bought
catch	caught
choose	chose
come	came
cost	cost
cut	cut
draw	drew
drink	drank
drive	drove
eat	ate
fall	fell
feel	felt
fight	fought
find	found
fly	flew
get	got
give	gave
go	went
grow	grew
hear	heard
hurt	hurt
keep	kept
know	knew

Base form	Past form
let	let
lose	lost
make	made
mean	meant
meet	met
pay	paid
put	put
read	read
ride	rode
run	ran
say	said
see	saw
sell	sold
sing	sang
sleep	slept
speak	spoke
swim	swam
take	took
teach	taught
tell	told
think	thought
throw	threw
understand	understood
wear	wore
win	won
write	wrote

WORD LIST

Word	Unit	Word	Unit	Word	Unit
horse	5	million	4	pop music	6
hungry	7	modern	8	practice	1
hurt	8	movie theater	10	practicing the violin	9
ice hockey	1	museum	10	prepare	12
ill	5	mustache	2	put on	3
immediately	10	near	10	put up decorations	12
improve	1	nearly	12	quick	5
in a row	3	nervous	11	raise money	12
in trouble	5	next to	10	rap	6
incredible	5	offer	10	recover	8
ingredient	12	orange	7	recycling	12
insect	4	order	12	red hair	2
instrument	6	origami	1	rescue	5
interested	11	pain	8	restaurant	10
jacket	3	pants	3	ride	9
jazz music	6	park	10	risk	11
jeans	3	park a car	10	rock music	6
job	5	parrot	5	rural	3
knee	8	patient	8	salty	7
leg	8	perform	6	school fair	12
lifelike	2	pet	5	search	5
long hair	2	pick someone up	9	serve	12
look after	8	pick up trash	12	share a pizza	11
look like	2	place	4	share an interest	11
lose	4	plan a charity event	12	shoes	3
main course	12	plane	11	short hair	2
meat	7	planet	4	shoulder-length hair	2
milk	7	plastic	12	sick	5

CREDITS

Photo Credits

Cover Beau Pilgrim, **4** (tl1) Design Pics, Inc./National Geographic Image Collection; (tl2) (tl3) JohnnyGreig/E+/Getty Images; (cl1) loreanto/Shutterstock.com; (cl2) VichoT/iStock/Getty Images; (bl1) Betty LaRue/Alamy Stock Photo; (bl2) PYMCA/Universal Images Group/Getty Images, **5** (tl1) Matthieu Paley/National Geographic Image Collection; (tl2) Halfpoint/Shutterstock.com; (cl1) Jeff R Clow/Moment/Getty Images; (cl2) © Marco Bottigelli/Moment/Getty Images; (bl1) Ken Fisher/The Image Bank/Getty Images; (bl2) Alistair Berg/Iconica/Getty Images, **6–7** Design Pics, Inc./National Geographic Image Collection, **7** (tl) Fresh_Studio/Shutterstock.com; (tc) Abeadev/Shutterstock.com; (tr) (cl) (c) Bioraven/Shutterstock.com, **9** Robyn Mackenzie/Shutterstock.com, **10** Mya–Rose Craig AKA Birdgirl, **12–13** Michael Gruber/Getty Images Entertainment/Getty Images, **13** Nick Wilkinson/Birmingham Mail, **15** (tr) Bob Bretall; (br) YummyBuum/Shutterstock.com, **16** Iain Masterton/Alamy Stock Photo, **18** JohnnyGreig/E+/Getty Images, **19** (c1) (c2) (c3) JohnnyGreig/E+/Getty Images, **21** David Schaffer/Caiaimage/Getty Images, **22** Imagine China/Newscom, **24** Tristan Gregory/Camera Press/Redux, **25** Ilona Studre/ullstein bild/Getty Images, **27** Radmila/Shutterstock.com, **28** (tl) (tc1) (tc2) (tc3) (tr) fredrisher/Shutterstock.com, **28–29** Jan Hetfleisch/Getty Images News/Getty Images, **29** YummyBuum/Shutterstock.com, **30–31** loreanto/Shutterstock.com, **31** (tl) Andromina/Shutterstock.com; (tc) (tr) Bioraven/Shutterstock.com; (c) Andromina/Shutterstock.com; (cl) (cr) Bioraven/Shutterstock.com; (bc) Bioraven/Shutterstock.com; (bl1) Andromina/Shutterstock.com; (bl4) Andromina/Shutterstock.com; (bl5) Bioraven/Shutterstock.com, **33** BeylaBalla/iStock/Getty Images, **34** janzgrossetkino/Moment/Getty Images, **36–37** Olek/Shutterstock.com, **38** Casey Kelbaugh/The New York Times/Redux, **39** (br1) Westend61/Getty Images; (br2) NoDenmand/Shutterstock.com, **40–41** ValentynVolkov/iStock/Getty Images, **42–43** VichoT/iStock/Getty Images, **45** (cl1) idreamphoto/shutterstock.com; (cl2) Interpix/Alamy Stock Photo; (cr1) Chris Hill/Shutterstock.com; (cr2) Bluedogroom/Shutterstock.com, **46** Amos Chapple/Shutterstock.com, **47** Elizabeth M. Ruggiero/iStock/Getty Images, **48–49** De Agostini/Universal Images Group/Alamy Stock Photo, **49** Staffan Widstrand/NPL/Minden Pictures, **51** jahmaica/iStock/Getty Images, **52–53** Cavan Images/Offset/Shutterstock.com, **54–55** Betty LaRue/Alamy Stock Photo, **58** Alan Vernon/Moment/Getty Images, **59** (bl) natrot/Shutterstock.com; (br) OlesyaNickolaeva/Shutterstock.com, **60–61** CB2/ZOB/WENN.com/Newscom, **62** Sasiistock/iStock/Getty Images, **63** (cr) Holger Leue/Lonely Planet Images/Getty Images; (b) Grigorenko/iStock/Getty Images; (br) Kudryashka/Shutterstock.com, **64–65** Juniors Bildarchiv GmbH/Alamy Stock Photo, **66–67** PYMCA/Universal Images Group/Getty Images, **67** (tl1) Marish/Shutterstock.com; (tl2) (cl1) Bioraven/Shutterstock.com; (cl2) (bl1) (bl2) Marish/Shutterstock.com, **69** Leren Lu/The Image Bank/Getty Images, **70** RGB Ventures/SuperStock/Alamy Stock Photo, **72–73** Mike Blake/Reuters, **74** Robyn Mackenzie/Shutterstock.com, **75** (br1) NoDenmand/Shutterstock.com; (br2) Christian Bertrand/Shutterstock.com, **76–77** Lev Fedoseyev/ITAR–TASS News Agency/Alamy Stock Photo, **78–79** Matthieu Paley/National Geographic Image Collection, **82** jacoblund/iStock/Getty Images, **84–85** © Dan DeLong Photography, **87** (cr1) nevodka/Shutterstock.com; (cr2) Evgeny Karandaev/Shutterstock.com; (cr3) Yalcin Sonat/Shutterstock.com; (cr4) Roman Samokhin/Shutterstock.com, **88–89** Dieter Heinemann/Shutterstock.com, **90–91** Halfpoint/Shutterstock.com, **91** (tl) (tc) (tr) (c) bsd/Shutterstock.com; (bl) Rvector/Shutterstock.com; (br) HN Works/Shutterstock.com, **93** Africa Studio/Shutterstock.com, **94** Kateryna Kon/Science Photo Library/Getty Images, **95** (t) Albert999/Shutterstock.com; (tr) MuchMania/Shutterstock.com, **96–97** Fritz Hoffmann/Redux, **98** Food Impressions/Shutterstock.com, **99** Kudryashka/Shutterstock.com, **100–101** Jordi Elias Grassot/Alamy Stock Photo, **102–103** Jeff R Clow/Moment/Getty Images, **105** (br) Vesnaandjic/E+/Getty Images, **106** Sophie Chivet/Agence VU'/Redux, **107** Johner Images/Getty Images; **108** Christoph Otto (www.christoph–otto.com), **109** Beawiharta/Reuters, **111** natrot/Shutterstock.com, **112** Kat Keene Hogue/National Geographic Image Collection, **114–115** Marco Bottigelli/Moment/Getty Images, **115** (tl) miri019/Shutterstock.com; (tc) (tr) bioraven/Shutterstock.com; (bl) (bc) (br) bioraven/Shutterstock.com, **118** Cameron Davidson/Corbis Documentary/Getty Images, **119** ©National Geographic Maps, **120** John B Hewitt/Alamy Stock Photo, **123** (c) Dragan Milovanovic/Shutterstock.com, **124** (tl) (tc)(tr) Clare Trainor/National Geographic Image Collection; (br) Nikada/E+/Getty Images, **126–127** Ken Fisher/The Image Bank/Getty Images, **129** svetikd/E+/Getty Images, **130** Lee Balterman/The Life Picture Collection/Getty Images, **131** (bl1) (bl2) TonyMeeHey/Shutterstock.com; (bl3) Kapreski/Shutterstock.com; (bl4) WonderfulPixel/Shutterstock.com; (bl5) Bioraven/Shutterstock.com; (bl6) (bl7) TonyMeeHey/Shutterstock.com; (br1) AVS–Images/Shutterstock.com; (br2) SSwasdee/Shutterstock.com; (br3) Leremy/Shutterstock.com; (br4) Azaze11o/Shutterstock.com; (br5) Kovalov Anatolii/Shutterstock.com, **132–133** Jeffrey Rotman/Biosphoto/Minden Pictures, **135** (br1) Charles Brutlag/Shutterstock.com; (br2) Lapina/Shutterstock.com, **136–137** Ekspansio/E+/Getty Images, **138–139** Alistair Berg/Iconica/Getty Images, **141** Richard Levine/Alamy Stock Photo, **142** (t) Natural History Archive/Alamy Stock Photo; (bl1) Mark Ji Sun/Shutterstock.com; (bl2) Zaur Rahimov/Shutterstock.com; (bc) RedlineVector/Shutterstock.com; (br) Azar Shikhaliyev/Shutterstock.com, **144** Brian Finke/National Geographic Image Collection, **146** natrot/Shutterstock.com, **147** (br1) ATU Images/Photographer's Choice/Getty Images; (br2) SVStudio/Shutterstock.com, **148–149** Leon Neal/AFP/Getty Images, **149** YummyBuum/Shutterstock.com, **150** JohnnyGreig/E+/Getty Images.

Art Credits

8, 20, 32, 44, 56, 68, 80, 92, 104, 116, 128, 140 (t) Ed Hammond/Deborah Wolfe Ltd, **83** (b), **117** (c), **151** (b) Peter Bull Art Studio, **81, 153, 154** (t) Lachina

Text Credits

25 Adapted from "We Are Actually Wax!" by Zachary Petit: NGK, Feb 2012, **97** Adapted from How Ancient Remedies Are Changing Modern Medicine" by Peter Gwin: NGM, Oct 2018, **133** Adapted from "Viral Photo of Great White Shark Stirs Debate Over Cages, Baiting" by Brian Clark Howard: National Geographic News, Oct 2014, **145** Adapted from "How 'Ugly' Fruits and Vegetables Can Help Solve World Hunger" by Elizabeth Royte: NGM, Mar 2016

ACKNOWLEDGMENTS

Thank you to the educators who provided invaluable feedback during the development of *Time Zones:*

ADVISORS

Apryl Peredo, Teacher, Hongo Junior and Senior High School, Tokyo
Carolina Espinosa, Coordinator, Associação Cultural Brasil-Estados Unidos, Brazil
Chary Aguirre, Academic and English Coordinator, Colegio Muñoz, Mexico
Elizabeth Yonetsugi, Global Program Manager, Berlitz Japan, Tokyo
Helena Mesquita Bizzarri, Academic Coordinator, SESI, Brazil
Hiroyo Noguchi, Lecturer, Momoyama Gakuin University (St. Andrew's University), Osaka
Isabella Alvim, Academic Coordinator, Instituto Brasil-Estados Unidos (IBEU) - Rio de Janeiro, Brazil
Kota Ikeshima, Teacher, Shibuya Junior & Senior High School, Tokyo
Nelly Romero, Head of Academic Design and Projects, Instituto Cultural Peruano Norteamericano (ICPNA), Peru
Nhi Nguyen, Program Manager, Vietnam USA Society English Centers (VUS), Ho Chi Minh City
Sabrina Hong, Education and Training Manager, Aston English, Xi'an
Sean Patterson, Global Programs Manager, Kanto Gakuin Mutsuura Junior and Senior High School, Yokohama
Sílvia de Melo Caldas, Course Designer, Casa Thomas Jefferson, Brazil
Sophy Oum, Academic Coordinator, ACE Cambodia, Phnom Penh
Wenjing Luo, Research and Development Manager, CERNET Education, Beijing
Yu-Chih (Portia) Chang, Head Teacher, Start Education Experts, Taipei

REVIEWERS

LATIN AMERICA

Adriene Zigaib, Brazil
Ana Paula Marques Migliari, School Connect, Brazil
Anna Lúcia Seabra Mendes, Casa Thomas Jefferson, Brazil
Auricea Bacelar, Top Seven Idiomas, Brazil
Barbara Souza, EM Maria Quiteria, Brazil
Daniela Coelho, SayOk! English School, Brazil
Gilberto Dalla Verde Junior, Colégio Tomas Agostinho, Brazil
Isabella Campos, Instituto Brasil-Estados Unidos (IBEU) - Rio de Janeiro, Brazil
Jessica Yanett Carrillo Torres, John Nash School, Peru
Juliana Pinho, Instituto Brasil-Estados Unidos (IBEU), Brazil
Juliana Ribeiro Lima Passos, CIEP 117 Carlos Drummond de Andrade Brasil-USA, Brazil
Katherin Ortiz Torres, Santa Angela Merici School, Peru
Kathleen Isabelle Tavares da Silva, Inglês Para Todos, Brazil
Larissa Pizzano Platinetti Vieira, Centro Cultural Brasil - Estados Unidos (CCBEU) Guarapuava, Brazil
Laura Raffo Pires, Extra English, Brazil
Luis Sergio Moreira da Silva, Webster, Brazil
María del Rosario Aguirre Román, Colegio Muñoz, Mexico
Maria Helena Querioz e Lima, Cultura Inglesa Uberlândia, Brazil
Mónica Rosales, Instituto Franklin de Veracruz, Mexico
Natasha Freitas Silva, ATW English, Brazil
Natasha Pereira, ATW English, Brazil
Neri Zabdi Barrenechea Garcia, Welcome English, Peru
Patricia Perez, Colégio Martin Miguel de Guemes, Argentina
Raphael Fonseca Porto, Casa Thomas Jefferson, Brazil
Renata Lucia Cardoso, Instituto Natural de Desenvolvimento Infantil, Brazil
Roosevelt Oliveira, Coopling, Brazil
Samuel Nicacio Silva Santos, Casa Thomas Jefferson, Brazil
Silvia Castilho Cintra, Ingles com Silvia, Brazil
Silvia Martínez Marín, I.E.P. Henri La Fontaine, Peru
Stela Foley, Brazil

EUROPE AND AFRICA

Theresa Taylor, American Language Center, Morocco

ASIA

Andrew Duenas, ILA Vietnam, Ho Chi Minh City
Camille Nota, Berlitz Japan, Tokyo
Dan Quinn, Jakarta Japanese School, Jakarta
Edwin G Wiehe, Shitennoji Junior and Senior High School, Osaka
Georges Erhard, ILA Vietnam, Ho Chi Minh City
Haruko Morimoto, Kanda Gaigo Career College, Tokyo
Mai Thị Ngọc Anh, ILA Vietnam, Ho Chi Minh City
Masaki Aso, Japan University of Economics, Fukuoka
Paul Adams, Ming Dao High School, Taichung
Samuel Smith, Jakarta Japanese School, Jakarta
Sayidah Salim, Dian Didatika Junior High School, Jakarta
Shogo Minagawa, Doshisha Junior High School, Kyoto
Trevor Goodwin, IBL English, Wonju
Yoko Sakurai, Aichi University, Nagoya